Hello God

By JJ Vasquez

To Liz

My parents helped me believe I could do *almost* anything.

Then I met you.

And the *almost* went away.

CONTENTS

PART 1

HELLO

VASQUEZ

CHAPTER 1

THE "INTRODUCTION"

"Christianity begins where religion ends...with the resurrection."

– Herbert Booth Smith

It makes no sense — yet it makes perfect sense.

"75% of Millennials who have dropped out of church say they have never heard Jesus speak to them in a personal way."

Think about it . . . To be labeled a church "drop out" implies that you were once a church "goer." That means that in some way, shape, or form, you were a regular participant in church – even if only in attendance.

That means you came on Sunday, week after week, to a building covered in images of Jesus, sang songs to Jesus, listened to sermons about Jesus, read stories about Jesus, with Jesus' *actual* words in red ink (so that you can't possibly miss them) – but then left, because you never heard Jesus speak.

How is that possible? It makes no sense. Either you're lying *or the Church is.*

"And if Christ has not been raised from the dead, your faith is mere delusion, futile, and fruitless…" - 1 Corinthians 15:17 AMP

Have you ever noticed that it's a resurrected Jesus that's preached every Sunday morning? A *resurrected* Jesus – as in not dead – as in *alive?* We've lost the implications of that statement, so humor me as I provide the definition of alive, to feel the weight of it.

*Alive: having life; living; existing; not dead or lifeless; in a state of action; full of energy and spirit; aware and interested; **responsive.***

Responsive – as in *speaks.*

Jesus is alive! That was the message of our spiritual forefathers. People believed, because that message was backed up by an active display of the Holy Spirit's power. Jesus is not an image on a stained glass window, or the protagonist of a religious fairy tale. He's the *living, acting, speaking* God of the Universe.

Albert Einstein's definition of insanity is doing the same thing, over and over again, and expecting different results. If that's true then today's generation of young people would have to be insane to keep coming to Church, Sunday after Sunday, week after week, to talk to a God who doesn't talk back. If we demonstrate that all He is, is a silent symbol, or an unresponsive historical figure (as suggested by the above statistic), then what other choice do we give them *but* to leave? Why would they keep coming? If He's not moving or speaking, then the church is lying. The Bible is false. Pastors are frauds. Jesus is dead.

It wasn't the empty tomb that convinced Mary Magdalene that Jesus was alive. In spite of all she saw and heard throughout the years of ministry with Jesus, when she first arrived at the garden and saw that the stone was rolled away, she didn't celebrate that Christ had risen - she cried for fear that his body had been stolen. It was only after *running into Jesus* on the way out of the garden, when she heard him say her name, "Mary" (John 20:16), that she believed. It was her *encounter* with the living God that convinced her.

For millions of teenagers and young adults, I fear what church has become - *an empty tomb with no encounter.* So like Mary, they walk away weeping – disappointed, disillusioned, and disinterested.

As a Professor of Youth and Family Ministry at one of the fastest growing Universities in the nation, my schedule is full of meetings with scholars and pastors who are desperately seeking a solution; they want to plant faith in the youth of their communities and churches. As a Youth Pastor of one of the nation's larger youth groups, I routinely sit across from mothers and fathers, who - with tears in their eyes - ask me why their child no longer wants to come to church. And as the parents of Justice and Zane, my wife and I have spent more nights than we can remember, lying in bed whispering over the hopes and fears of where our boys will spend eternity.

I've read the books, attended the conferences, and sat in strategy sessions with preeminent denominational leaders and some of the most brilliant minds in ministry today. What I share with you in the upcoming chapters is the product of all my research and personal experience from ministering to students for over a decade. This is the secret to keeping and reaching the next generation for Christ:

They have to hear Him speak.

So faith comes from hearing, and hearing what comes…from the lips of Christ himself. – Romans 10:17 AMP

The Greek word that Paul uses here is *"rhema."* It literally means "utterance" – that which is or has been uttered by a living voice. A *living* voice. Faith is born in the life of a young person the day she hears Jesus speak her name, the day she runs into Him.

You Can't Say Hallelujah…Until You Say Hello

Over the last decade, much research has been done on this "next generation" and whether or not the church will be relevant to them. The fear is, that in the midst of this YouTube, iTunes, Instagram, information-heavy world that church has lost, or at least is losing, its appeal. And in response to this fear were born the "Starbucks," "night club," and just plain "cool" churches of the world. Now, to be clear, I have no problem with these churches. They're great. The vibes, lights, and atmospheres make church better. Like vacations, home-cooked meals, and throwing out the trash make marriage better. But these things don't *make* marriage. My wife makes my marriage. And those things don't *make* the church. Jesus makes church.

To be clear – not the knowledge of, stories of, images of, or prophecies of Jesus. *Jesus.* I'm talking about the person of Christ made known through an encounter with the presence of his Holy Spirit. It's in this divine encounter where religion evolves into relationship.

Is Church no longer relevant to this millennial generation? Is it not cool enough? Has it finally become too opposed to the cultural norms? Or is it simply unbelievable?

No. We've just misjudged what this generation wants out of church and out of God. Not entertainment, not happiness, not relevance, or even (God forgive me) eternal security. All they want and *all they need* – is to hear Him speak.

They want to know God. They want to hear God. They want to talk to God. Like going on a blind date, the hard part isn't asking this generation of young people to connect with a God they have not seen, *but rather asking them to love a God they have not met.*

You can't love someone you've never met. You can work for them, sure. But you can't love them. A young person doesn't want to be God's employee. And they're not called to be. They want to be his children. They want a relationship.

This is where we miss it. We build our strategies around the idea that we're supposed to get young people to serve God, to obey God, and to praise God. When really, all that comes out of first *loving* God.

Because you can't say hallelujah until you say "hello".

Abraham said "Hello" at Haran, Moses said it at Horeb, Jacob at Bethel, Paul on the road to Damascus, and I said "Hello" at a Youth Camp in the mountains of Pennsylvania. Every believer, before they can truly believe, has to encounter God. All authentic relationships begin with an introduction. And in God's case - He makes one heck of an introduction.

Call it what you want: an encounter, an infilling, a baptism, a divine collision. In this book, we'll call it a *"meeting."* Because that's really what it is. Each biblical individual mentioned above, at one point in their lives, had a supernatural, personal meeting with the maker of Heaven and Earth. In that moment, God was internally promoted from concept to Creator, from myth to Majesty, and from tradition to Truth.

The end goal of this book is not to shape your theology, but to give you the tried and tested tools to create the environments that encourage encounters; to "set up" the meeting with God and our youth. It was written for anybody who believes that the hope of our world is not found in politics or presidents, better laws or schools, but in raising up a generation of passionate Christ followers. No, it will not guarantee that your children get to Heaven or that revival breaks out in your city. *But it's your best shot at both.*

We can't afford to wait. Time is too valuable, we must act now. If you share my concern for the next generation, know that the most important thing you can do isn't to *tell* them about Jesus, but to *introduce* them to him. He's lived in stories long enough. It's time they met Him.

It's time to say "Hello."

VASQUEZ

CHAPTER 2

RUNAWAY BRIDE

Maggie: I wanted to tell you why I run – sometimes ride – away from things.

Ike: Does it matter?

Maggie: I think so. [takes a deep breath]

Maggie: When I was walking down the aisle, I was walking toward somebody who didn't have any idea who I really was. And it was only half the other person's fault, because I had done everything to convince him that I was exactly what he wanted. So it was good that I didn't go through with it because it would have been a lie.

[pauses]

Maggie: But you – you knew the real me.

Ike: Yes, I did.

– Julia Roberts, *"Runaway Bride"*

The year was 1998. The snow was falling that night, powdering the streets of New York enough to bring it to life, but not enough to shut it down. On a typical school night I would have more than welcomed a snow day, but not today. Tomorrow was special. Although December typically has two nights worth staying up late for, this was neither. I couldn't sleep for another reason.

I was 12 years old and my parents were volunteer youth pastors at a small Spanish church in Brooklyn. Every year around the same time, they would pack the church van full of students (and by "full" I mean 10 students) and drive 3 hours north of the city to the mountains of Pennsylvania, where thousands of teenagers and young adults gathered to listen to inspiring sermons, sing songs, and even though it wasn't supposed to be the focus - maybe keep an eye out for the pretty girl or cute guy that loves Jesus as much as they did.

In our church, youth ministry started at 12 years old, and having only recently turned 12, you can imagine how excited I was to finally get the chance to attend. Every year, I had to hear from the older kids about how great it was, and how awesome the sermons were, and how hot the girls were. I mean - how powerful the services were. I was ecstatic! I didn't know what to expect, but my expectations were high. I packed up for the weekend, and became student #11.

When we arrived at the hotel, my excitement grew even more as students from all over the northeastern United States greeted us. So we rushed out the van, unloaded our bags, checked in, and got ready for the first service of the weekend. My guy friends and I proceeded to apply absurd amounts of hair gel and cologne, grabbed our Bibles (back when Bibles didn't light up), and left for the convention center.

It's Not What You Think

It really isn't. But reading my story from your perspective, I can see how you'd be misled. You see a kid so excited about going to Church camp that he can't sleep the night before - a pre-teen from a good home, with good parents who love God. Not to mention, he's carrying a Bible. In one sense, you're right, I was a "good kid." But, if you're thinking I believed in God, or loved him for that matter, you are gravely mistaken. And if you work or live with young people, they might not be what you think they are either.

I mean sure, being a voluntary youth leader's son did come with some basic Bible knowledge and better-than-average church involvement. I was that kid in Sunday school class who always had the answer to the teacher's questions. I was a proud member of our youth ministry's drama team. I knew all the worship songs, in English and in Spanish. I prayed three times a day, although it usually coincided with meals and sounded something like, "Jesus, thank you for my food. Amen." I could even recite Psalms 23 from heart (thanks to the hip-hop song, "Gangsta's Paradise," by Coolio). But most importantly, as far as I knew, I was saved.

I'm pretty sure that at some point in my adolescence (though I can't remember when) I invited Jesus to live inside my heart and to wash away all my sins. If you asked me then if I believed in God, I would absolutely have said yes. But if that's your definition of a

Christian, then it's not what you think.

Christians are not "good" people. At least, not in the way that some people think. You're not a Christian because you're an outstanding citizen, or because your vocabulary is profanity-free. Or because you read your Bible or go to a Church camp. In fact, going to Church doesn't make you a Christian any more than going to the beach makes you a starfish. Church is something Christians practice, and an important one at that, but it's not what makes you a Christian *or* even a good person. In a radical redefinition of righteousness, the Bible teaches that it isn't a reward reserved for the religious, *but for those in relationship*.

Looking back on my childhood, I can see now that I never had anything even close to resembling a relationship with God. The power of religion is what got me to church every Sunday morning. Or in my context, the power of a whooping! In my house, Church wasn't a choice. We didn't have an option to sleep in (on one of the two days we didn't have to wake up early for school). My sister and I were going to go to Church, and we were going to like it. Unless you were bleeding, throwing up, or unable to control your bodily functions, you knew where to be on Sunday.

My parents were tough, but they had good intentions. They were Christians and they wanted me to be a Christian too. They loved Jesus, and they wanted me to love him too. They succeeded - at half of it.

They were able to raise me in Christianity, because Christianity is a religion. The prerequisite is knowledge, something I got plenty of in church and at home. But, they couldn't make me love Him, because love is a choice. The prerequisite is a relationship. I would grow up knowing all about Jesus, but never *knowing* Jesus. As much as they tried, this wasn't love; it was an arranged marriage.

I Do?

I once met a girl in college who was in an arranged marriage. I remember being overcome with curiosity during some downtime while working on a group project. Showing as much respect to her culture as possible, I asked, "What's it like to marry someone you don't know?"

I could tell by the swiftness of her response that this wasn't the first time she'd been asked, because she quickly corrected me, "But I do know him."

I paused in confusion, thinking for a second that maybe I didn't know what an arranged marriage was. Then she continued, "His name is _____. He's 5 feet 8 inches tall, he has black hair, his parents are doctors, he wants to be a doctor, and he loves politics."

Wow, she was right. She knew him. Or at least *about* him. Feeling like she missed what I was trying to ask, I rephrased the question to more accurately represent the spirit of my inquiry.

"Ok, but...how does it feel to marry someone *you've never met?*" And then that got me thinking: *I wonder how many Christians carry on this same tradition?*

If you grew up in church, I bet I could recreate the day you got "saved," give or take a few details. One day, when you were young, a parent\preacher\pastor grabbed your attention and said,

"Let me tell you about Jesus! You'll love him, He's awesome! He's nice, kind, forgiving, loving, protecting - a really great guy! You should give him your life."

You responded, "Umm, Ok! Sounds cool. Why not? *I'll give him the rest of my life.*" Then you raised your hand, or went to the front of the church, and repeated a prayer. Just like that, you entered into a "committed relationship" with Christ.

I bet that by that time you could've told me a lot about him: that he was born in a manger under a star, to a mother named Mary, with three old guys standing by, and some kid playing a drum. That he lived a perfect life, healed a bunch of people, gave good advice, died on a cross, and then rose from the dead. Wow. You know a lot about him. Which is great if you're studying for a test. *But not so helpful if you're walking down the aisle.*

In the Spanish language, we actually have two different verbs for the one English verb "to know": *saber* and *conocer*. If I were to ask, "Do you know who my wife is?" I would use the verb *saber*. I would use that word, because I'm asking you a question with an answer that's factual: true or false. You could respond, "Yes. Her name is Liz."

But if I wanted to ask you, "Do you *know* my wife?" I would use the verb *conocer*. I would use that word, because I'm asking you a question with an answer that is experiential. To use the verb *conocer* requires more than knowledge; it demands an encounter. I have friends on Facebook, who live on other continents, who can answer the first question. But, you can't answer the second question unless you meet her.

It's impossible to grow up in church and not know about God, but it's all too common to grow up in church and never know God. In one sense, every Christian is "walking down the aisle." The book of Revelation in the Bible speaks of the Bride being made ready. Christians are that Bride. One day, we'll get to the altar and spend eternity with Christ.

Jesus has done the work for us, eternal salvation isn't hard, it's free. Our only job is to continue to walk towards Christ, as a bride walks toward the groom. But there's many days between this day and that. And somewhere along this walk, the reality of commitment sets in. The reality that being in a relationship with Christ will be difficult, that we give up all other suitors in the monogamy of salvation, and not to mention the sacrifice and persecution (which is something the pastor conveniently left out when he offered you Jesus).

At this point, the young person raised in Church will begin to think: "Wait a minute, what am I doing? I don't even know this guy! I got dressed and started walking, because that's what was expected of me. It's a decision my parents made for me." And, "I've been playing a part this whole time - knowing what was expected of me, I pretended to be someone I'm not. *He doesn't even know the real me.*" Then, they book it for the chapel doors.

The Day I Met Him

I would say that's where I was on the first service of Church camp that December evening - a runaway bride. I knew what my parents wanted. I knew what God wanted. But, there was no way I could see this Church thing through, because I still didn't know what I wanted. "Jesus loves you", they said. But, they never bothered to ask if I loved Him. Maybe because deep down inside they knew I couldn't.

I remember the day I came home bragging about my first girlfriend, and what my dad told me, "You're too young to know what love is." What he was really saying was, "You haven't been through much, son. You don't have enough experience." It was good advice when I was dating, but I probably could've used it in my faith as well. Because it wasn't until that first night at the convention center that I realized I didn't. It wasn't until after that night that I did.

After a moving time of worship at the Church camp, the guest speaker took the stage. I can't tell you what he preached about, what the altar call was for, what song was playing, or who prayed for me. What I do remember was my emptiness, a feeling that what I needed was at the altar. Like a newborn turtle instinctively turns to the sea, I didn't know what awaited me, yet with the powerful combination of fear, excitement, and desperation, I knew that was where I needed to be. So I ran, closed my eyes, and waited. Somebody began to pray for me, and that was it. That was the day I met Him.

I can't explain what happened. Most attempts at explaining personal supernatural or spiritual experiences come off as spooky or weird, so I won't even try. But maybe Paul described it best,

"The Spirit searches all things…for who knows a person's thoughts except their own spirit within them? In the same way no one knows the thoughts of God except the Spirit of God."
(1 Corinthians 2:10-11).

This is what I mean by encounter.
This is meeting God: to know and be known by Him.

Even as I type these words, the edges of my mouth curl with a grin of reminiscence, just like when I talk about the day I met Liz. No, I wasn't perfect after that day. I doubted again after that day. I would run from God again and again after that day. But, I left that day with something greater than any failure, doubt or religion, something all great relationships have in common, and something my parents could never give me…

I left with my own story.

VASQUEZ

Chapter 3

GOD DOESN'T HAVE GRANDKIDS

"I am tired of reading about God's visitations of yesteryear. I want God to breakout somewhere in my lifetime, so that in the future my children can say, "I was there. I know; it's true." God has no grandchildren. Each generation must experience His presence."

– Tommy Tenney

I was reading the most random and abrupt Facebook message ever. Partly because my dad was new to the whole social media scene, so I really didn't expect a post at all, never mind what was coursing across my screen:

"Just found out that my father passed away in January of this year. Not sure what I'm feeling. A little confused, sad, mad, I went to see him in New Jersey because I wanted to say good bye (didn't get that chance)."

He wrote that in November, ten months after his passing.

Why, you might ask, was there such a great disconnect between father and son? Here's a brief bio on my grandfather: he was evil. A very abusive and violent man who spent more time in the bars and jail cells of New York than at home. Here's a brief bio on my dad: he's the second oldest of 10 siblings, all with the same parents. And one night while my grandfather was out drinking, the entire family packed what they could carry, then literally ran for their lives.

Now I wont bother you with the horror stories my father shared with me of what it was like growing up in that home. You have enough context to understand the tension between the two of them. I understand why he felt the way he did. What was tough for me was figuring out why *I* felt the way *I* did. I had just heard through social media that my grandpa died, and I, like my father, was confused, but for completely different reasons.

On one hand, my grandfather had died. A man responsible for me being on this planet, a man whose last name I carry.

But on the other hand, I don't have the history with him that my father did. Can you believe I've never even seen a picture of the guy? Every bit of information I have was passed down to me. Granted, it was enough to make me dislike him, but even my dislike wasn't authentic. I knew what I should've felt. I should've felt angry. I should've felt sad. I should've felt upset. But, I couldn't, because I'd never met him.

Any authentic emotional response was limited, because I had never personally encountered him. I'm not saying that he wasn't as bad as they say he was. My point is: love and hate are emotions you can never experience through another person's story.

Don't get me wrong. It's not that stories aren't powerful - they are. But, someone else's story will never mean more to you than your own. Sad movies can make you cry, and funny movies can make you laugh, but a death in your immediate family can lead to depression, and a birth can lead to smiles that last a lifetime.

My dad's stories were as moving as a "made-for-TV" movie, but they were still *his* stories. Like the joy you feel "for" the hero and the anger you feel "at" the villain in your favorite movie, the emotions are really only skin deep. They're over by the time the credits roll. You don't hold a lifelong grudge against Cinderella's stepmom or the guy who shot Bambi's mother.

Sure, my dad's stories made me love him more, because I could appreciate where he came from. But, I spent my adolescence with him, so I had personal experience to go along with it. As far as my grandfather was concerned, my whole life I was practically indifferent towards him. I didn't really give him much thought. I never knew him. Fortunately, that means I could never truly hate him, despite his choices in life, and despite what he put my aunts and uncles through. It's not my story. On the flip side though, that also means I could never truly love him. I could print t-shirts with his face on them, rename my son after him, but it wouldn't make a difference. To love someone requires first-hand experience and sacrifice.

Secondhand Love

I think that, for a lot of teenagers, God is like that ancestor you hear about. The stories are powerful, emotions are elicited, and responses are expected. But, if you remember nothing else this chapter, remember this: *there is a generation attending church today that is vicariously in love with Jesus.*

Young people who try and fail at loving God, fail because their response is limited by their encounters. So, they cling to others' stories, suggesting what they should feel, hoping that they could feel. But it's impossible.

There's no such thing as secondhand love.

No matter how many "God stories" (biblical or personal) a student hears from pastors and parents, those stories can never birth genuine love, because it's not their story. Their connection to Christ is based on the knowledge of their fathers. They haven't met

Him for themselves.

It's like the story of the Samaritan woman, whose life changes after encountering Jesus at the community well. So much so that she runs off to her village to tell the rest of her neighbors the good news. While most are intrigued, *none are convinced*. Why? It was *her* story. She was the one that met God, not them. That is, until they met him for themselves.

Then they said to the woman, "Now we believe, <u>not just because of what you told us</u>, but because we have heard him ourselves. Now we know that he is indeed the Savior of the world." - John 4:42 NLT

"Not just because of what you told us..." Listen to that. This is the very real and harsh cry of a postmodern generation. They'll never believe "just because." They refuse to. They need a reason. They need an encounter. They're tired of sermons and exhortations. They need to meet Him for themselves.

The God of Your Father

"Call me Jacob," said the youth of today. I cannot help but notice the resemblances between the two. Both try to be someone they're not, both rather flee from their problems rather than face them, both wrestle with God, and both are destined. But most concerning, is that both only had knowledge of the Lord - never experience. While fleeing for his life after deliberately robbing his older brother of his inheritance, Jacob has a dream.

"At sundown he arrived at a good place to set up camp and stopped there for the night. Jacob found a stone to rest his head against and lay down to sleep. As he slept, he dreamed of a stairway that reached from the earth up to heaven. And he saw the angels of God going up and down the stairway. At the top of the stairway stood the LORD, and he said, "I am the LORD, the God of your grandfather Abraham, and the God of your father, Isaac." Genesis 28: 11–13 NLT

Notice the Lord's choice of words here: I am the God of "your grandfather," the God of "your father" - but what he doesn't say is the most significant: "*your* God". In other words, "Hello Jacob. I'm God, you don't know me, but I'm a friend of your dad's."

Why the introduction? If dads yesterday were anything like they are today, there's no doubt that Jacob was well aware of who God was. I could recount to you my father's childhood stories, as if they were my own, with every colorful detail. It's a fact of life that whether you want to hear it or not, if there's a story to tell, you know a dad's going to tell it. And it wasn't like Jacob's dad Isaac didn't have stories!

"One day your grandfather and I went for a hike, or at least that's what he told me we were doing. Then he tried to kill me. If Grandpa Abe ever asks you to go with him to 'worship,' make sure you bring the lamb first." Or, how about the famous, "how I met your mother" story? Who has a better one than Isaac?

There's no question that Jacob's childhood was heavily inundated with the history of the patriarchs, God's powerful promises to Abraham under the stars, and his own rags to riches blessings in Egypt. Just as my father shared the tragedies of his childhood, I imagine Isaac shared the miracles of his. Yet, when God introduces himself to Jacob, he does so as if it were the first time Jacob had ever heard of him. But it wasn't - *it was just the first time he'd ever met Him*. Jacob had knowledge of God, he just didn't know Him.

How many students in our churches, even our own children, can relate to Jacob? How many teenagers and young adults have heard about God through their fathers and grandfathers, but have never met Him themselves? How many have heard messages about the love of God, yet have never been wrapped by it? The peace of God, yet have never been filled with it? The cross, but have never carried it?

You can pass down religion, but you can't pass down relationship.

Repeat After Me

Every night I read the Bible and pray with my son, "Repeat after me: Dear God..." I feed him the words, because he's only three years old. He cares more about Spiderman and tigers than he does Jesus. I get that. I don't expect him to quote Scripture or call down fire from Heaven. I'm just trying to establish a model for him, a habit of relationship. I don't actually believe he's praying, because he's not. He's just repeating what I'm saying. But I do it anyway, because as a parent, I hope that one day I wont have to have him repeat me, that the words will be truly his, and the desire his as well.

The faith of our youth today is a lot like that. They follow the patterns that they see. They wake up in the morning, put on the "church clothes," go to youth group, sing the songs, and pray the prayers. It's a repetition of life. They're following the model laid out for them by their parents. They're repeating. And that's great, but that will only last as long as the model is mandated, as long as it's the norm, and as long as it's convenient.

This is why so many young adults leave church after high school. For them, church is a habit, the product of repetition - mechanical, dry, and emotionless repetition. But, for the person who meets God, church becomes so much more. In fact, it makes its greatest evolution possible: from a habit to a home.

"Home is where the heart is." In my ministry travels, I've learned that this saying has nothing to do with how much you love a location. I enjoy visiting New York City very much. Every time I'm there I have a great time visiting old friends and eating the best pizza on the planet (sorry Chicago). But, even though I was born there, I wouldn't call it home. Home is not a question of "where is it?" but rather "who's there?" Orlando is my home, because that's where my wife and kids are. Church is home, because in that place you encounter the presence of God. He meets you, he makes it personal, and your own story begins. Then you go to Church, and love it, because you know He's there.

Biting your nails, tapping your feet, picking your nose. Most people hate their habits; church shouldn't fall into this category.

And the only way to shift that categorization is through choice. A young person can't love God because he's been conditioned to. There has to be a genuine choice - made from a genuine heart - formed by a genuine encounter. You must "Taste and see that The Lord is good" (Psalms 34:8) for yourself, before truly ever buying in to Him.

One day, your faith will have to develop a "voice" of its own, it must have its own story to tell, and its own words to tell it. Or, you risk living life as an "echo," a fading repetition of your father's prayers. There's only one way to keep faith from fading, only one way to make sure young people hang in for life.

A lesson I learned the day I met Liz.

VASQUEZ

Chapter 4

ENCOUNTERING ENDURANCE

"'Who are you, sir?' I asked." And the Lord replied, 'I
am Jesus, the one you are persecuting.
Now stand up! For I have appeared to you to appoint
you as my servant and my witness.
You are to tell the world about this encounter...

– Acts 26:14-16

"Impossible."

"That someone could be this fine."

"AND love Jesus."

That was all I could think the day I first met my wife.

Though, technically, I don't think you could really call it "meeting." There wasn't any conversation per se, no handshake, not even the awkward eye contact from a distance that then shifted to the subtle smile. I was way too shy for that. Her beauty had nullified all the traditional tactics of approach. I didn't know what to do, but I couldn't help looking. So I did what any respectful young man would do: I followed her.

Don't judge me. Some might call that weird; others a crime, whatever. She was one of a kind, and I didn't know if I would ever see someone like her again. So, I followed her.

We were both at a youth convention in a hotel in Tampa, Florida. She left the service, I left the service. She went in the elevator, I went in the elevator. She got off on the 7th floor, I got off on the 7th floor. She went left, I went left. She walked into her room, I kept walking. Believe it or not, my first conversation with her wouldn't take place for another 3 years — but I was hooked. I remember running back down to the lobby to catch up with my best friend. "You would never believe what just happened! I just met the most beautiful girl in the world!"

This might sound made up, but I promise you, in that short encounter Liz had become the standard by which every girlfriend to follow would be measured. That moment changed me. Her beauty represented something far more than just a physical attraction. In that moment, it felt almost like a promise. Not a love-at-first-sight kind of thing, because I honestly had no idea that I would marry her nor was God telling me that. But, in my soul, a bar had been set. It was as if God was saying, "The person I have for you will make you feel like this girl made you feel, every day. So, don't settle, don't rush, be patient. I have the best saved for you."

In the dark times of my life that followed (and there were many), I endured. When I thought I'd never get married, that I'd always be alone and always be struggling, I remembered the girl with the curly blond hair. I remembered how she made me feel. But more importantly, I remembered what God had said. The moment was fleeting, but the promise enduring.

It was then when I learned that few things can instill endurance like an encounter.

Have you ever wondered what made Paul so committed? Even after all he went through? If you were to take a lesson on endurance from anyone, it'd be Paul of Tarsus. Check out his resume,

"I have worked harder, been put in prison more often, been whipped times without number, and faced death again and again. Five different times the Jewish leaders gave me thirty-nine lashes. Three times I was beaten with rods. Once I was stoned. Three times I was shipwrecked. Once I spent a whole night and a day adrift at sea. I have traveled on many long journeys. I have faced danger from rivers and from robbers. I have faced danger from my own people, the Jews, as well as from the Gentiles. I have faced danger in the cities, in the deserts, and on the seas. And I have faced danger from men who claim to be believers but are not. I have worked hard and long, enduring many sleepless nights. I have been hungry and thirsty and have often gone without food. I have shivered in the cold, without enough clothing to keep me warm." 2 Corinthians 11:23–27 NLT

How did he do it? Well, you can often tell how a person will finish by first understanding how he or she started. How did Paul start? He was knocked off his horse, heard a voice from heaven, and was blinded by God's glory.

"Who are you Lord? Then the Lord said, 'I am Jesus'" (Acts 9:5). Hello God. Hello Paul. This encounter shapes Paul's ministry and his calling. But most effectively, it instills within him an attitude of endurance. No matter what happens, he's not quitting. How could he? He met God.

"From Bible-Belt Pastor to Atheist Leader"

That was the title of a recent article in the *N.Y. Times*. I couldn't help but read on. Those headline editors were good. Surely, there were some "creative rights" taken here. Atheist *leader?* It was the true story of an evangelical minister, a native Texan, who had been pastoring for 25 years. One day, he received a call from a member of his church asking for prayer. Her brother had been in a terrible motorcycle accident and was near death; she was desperate for counsel.

After years of convincing his congregations that "God was in control," the pastor was no longer convinced. Right there and then, he decided that he could no longer believe it. Refusing to enact God in any way, he did the best he could to comfort the woman, then hung up, wept, and resigned his faith. Not wanting anyone to ever experience the pain he felt in that moment, he began to "out reach" to other ministers who were also struggling with their faith. Channeling his inner-preacher, he began to speak at conferences and forums linked by a network of ex-clergy. In little time, he rose to popularity in the world of "reverse-conversion," which is the process of leading people *away* from faith in God. He shares his insight with the *N.Y. Times* reporter.

When asked what the principal challenge was in "helping" a seasoned minister "de-convert," he informed the reporter that,

"The transition away from faith may start with an intellectual epiphany, but it runs through a difficult reinterpretation of your own past. For believers, this often involves the 'hook,' or *a miraculous story that helps anchor your faith.*"

Did you miss it? He said that every believer has a story, a miraculous one, and he or she will not be able to let go of their faith unless that story is dealt with, either rationalized or forgotten. If this generation could have their own story, they would have their anchor. How do you argue with someone who's met the miracle-making God? You can't. The Pharisees tried it once and were frustrated.

All I Know Is…

John chapter 9 tells the story of a man who was born blind, but then meets Jesus and was miraculously healed. When the Pharisees hear about what happened, they immediately summon the man to court to testify.

These religious leaders were quickly losing their influence in the community to Jesus. With every message preached and miracle performed, Jesus was gaining more followers. An ex-blind man going around telling everybody that Jesus healed him was bad for business. Nothing like that had ever been done in the history of Israel, not in the time of Moses, Samuel, or Elijah. The blind man's story was too powerful. So after convening amongst themselves, the Pharisees devised a strategy.

They had two plans of action:

1. Either prove that the blind man was a fraud and that this miracle was a hoax.
2. Or convince the blind man that what had happened had not really happened. Make him believe that he was mistaken, and that this supernatural encounter was something else, something more rational.

The first approach was to expose this tale as a hoax:

"The Jewish leaders wouldn't believe he had been blind, so they called in his parents. They asked them, 'Is this your son? Was he born blind? If so, how can he see?' His parents replied, 'We know this is our son and that he was born blind, but we don't know how he can see or who healed him.'" - John 9:18–21 NLT

First approach failed, the miracle was legit. So, on to Plan B.

The Pharisees thought to themselves, "Ok. The guy can see, and he couldn't see before. If we can't undo the miracle, let's at least try to undo the story. We have to get him to believe it didn't happen, that it couldn't possibly have happened."

"So for the second time they called in the man who had been blind and told him, 'Give glory to God by telling the truth, because we know Jesus is a sinner.'" - John 9:24

Frustrated by their attempts to persuade him, the man takes an inventory of his remaining options. What else can he say? What else can he do? The people who are arguing with him are smarter, better educated, more experienced, older, and more talented debaters. He begins to think that maybe they were right. Maybe he was crazy. The Pharisees had succeeded, the man was confused. Yet, they had also failed, because even in his confusion, he still had his story.

"'I don't know whether he is a sinner,' the man replied. '*But I know this:* I was blind, and now I can see!'" John 9:25

Like the Pharisees, the world is full of people who will try to convince this generation that Jesus is not who he said he was. They will argue, investigate, rationalize, and reject any and all evidence that says otherwise. But like the blind man, a generation filled with the Holy Spirit, who has encountered the supernatural presence of God, he has the high ground in this debate.

The scholars, celebrities, and pundits can discredit Jesus all they want, deny his power and authority, perhaps even His existence. But they can never take away the young man's story. Like the blind man, ill-equipped for debate, he'll respond, "I don't know…that's a good question…great point. "

"All I know is…I was blind, and now I see. All I know is…I met Him."

This reminds me of a story in Erwin Mcmanus' book *The Barbarian Way*. He and his son were driving home from church when, unbeknownst to Erwin, he was about to find out where his boy really stood with his faith.

Years later when Aaron was about fourteen, I saw this so clearly. We were driving in the car together and had one of those gut-wrenching heart-to-heart talks.

"Dad, I think that if I had not been raised in a Christian home, I would not be a Christian," he said.

You can imagine the rush of emotions going through me. It took all the restraint I had to not panic and stay calm.

"Why do you think that?" I asked as if his statement had no emotional effect on me.

Aaron continued, "I have way too many doubts and questions."

"Oh," I said, sounding as relieved as I could. "I have those too. So what are you going to do?"

I'll never forget Aaron's answer. It was one of the clearest confirmations that my son was not an unwilling member of a religion, that he, too, was a true barbarian. "Well, <u>I've met God</u>. So what are you supposed to do?"

To be clear: I'm not saying that a person doesn't doubt his or her beliefs after meeting God. You do. It's just that once you've met Him, doubt doesn't pull you away from God; it pulls you closer.

Benefit of the Doubt

I went to a secular university to study religion. I knew God had called me to ministry, but I wanted to hear about God from an outsider's perspective. I knew that what would be taught there would challenge my faith, but I looked forward to it. I wouldn't recommend this route for everyone, but I think at the time I needed someone to question my beliefs. I needed to be sure of my faith — but I had no idea what was in store.

My first class was Old Testament Scriptures. My professor walks in, and - without announcing it - it's clear to see that he is a proud member of the homosexual community. Now just so you know, I have two gay uncles and two gay aunts. I'm used to spending time with, and loving, people with different values. But none of them are experts in the Hebrew language!

Needless to say, this guy knew his stuff. He could point to practically any word in the Old Testament in English, and (without Google) tell you what the word was in Hebrew, along with the definition. His breadth of knowledge really impressed me, but it was his hermeneutics that took me for a ride.

He went on to give us his perspective on God and the Bible. Things I had never heard before. Ideas such as: The fall of man was a good thing (could you imagine life without clothes?), everything from Genesis to Deuteronomy was the imaginary history of a people group searching for an identity, and (no surprise here) King David was in a romantic relationship with his friend Jonathan. They were all silly ideas to any Sunday School church graduate like myself. Except, the professor backed up his arguments with cold, hard facts.

At the end of every class I would look at the other students who I recognized from churches in the area. And in their eyes you could see their faith dripping from their souls. It was as if our professor had exposed the brittleness of their "God tank" and it was starting to leak. He asked questions I couldn't answer. He tried to lead me and every student in that classroom away from faith in God, and many were. But, ironically, that class actually brought me so much closer. The professor would often ask, "How do you explain...?" and "But if that's true, then ..." or "What about...?"

I don't know.

But I met Him.

Convinced of my encounter with the creator of the universe, I was driven to deeper biblical depths than ever before, sure that there was treasure at the bottom. Did I doubt? Yes. But, because of my encounter, it only brought me closer. The professor's insistence had combined with my ignorance, but was still no match for the Holy Spirit's imminence.

Doubt tests your faith. Not like a teacher tests a student - to see how much they know - but, rather like an engineer tests a plane - to see how high they'll go.

So Let's Get Started…

Up until now, we've only been discussing the "why" behind encounter. Now, we move on to the "how." What you're about to read has taken me almost 2 years to put on paper. Describing encounter was hard (the last 4 chapters). But *prescribing* it? This is a task I approached with fear, awe, trembling, humility, and patience. I know that at this point some may consider what I have to say controversial; others will disagree, and some may be offended.

"How dare you put God in a box?" they'll think. "How dare you make a formula out of the mysterious?" they'll say.

I hear you. But please hear me. Keep reading, because I do nothing of the sort.

The process I'm going to share with you is founded in Scripture, tested in the field, and universal in application. It's centered on the idea of "Bethel," the place where Jacob met God, and where God became "his" God. It's the place where stories are written. And the best part about this place? You don't have to find a new pastor, a new family, or a new church to get there.

Because Bethels are built.

PART 2

BUILDING BETHELS

VASQUEZ

Chapter 5

BETHELS ARE BUILT

"God is still in the business of coming down to earth: to this cubicle, this email, this room, this house, this job, this hospital room, this car, this bed, this vacation. Any place can become bethel, the house of God. Or the chair you're sitting in as you read these words."

– John Ortberg

My son is a *huge* Mickey Mouse fan. Part of his affinity has to do with the fact that Liz and I live just over 20 minutes away from Disney World, and we recently became season ticket holders. That was *her* idea.

I wanted to wait until the kids were older. Our oldest, Justice, was only 2 years old when we got them, and I didn't think he would appreciate everything Disney had to offer quite yet. My wife had a good counter-argument: Kids under 2 years old get in free, and he was about to turn 3.

So…yea…we got the tickets.

And since then, every time we go, my son looks forward to one thing - meeting Mickey. Unfortunately, so do the other 50,000 kids at the park. So every trip, we wait for hours (which feels like days because they don't allow strollers in their lines - no point here - just venting) to see the mouse.

I remember the first time we took him, I wondered if he would even enjoy it, if we were wasting our time in this line. I feared that by the time we got to the end we would just be met with the tears and screams of a terrified 2 year old in the presence of a man-sized rodent. I mean, the only real previous "Mickey experience" he had was a stuffed toy that his Grandma got him. And he would play with it once in a while, but there was no real connection.

"Mickey is our thing." I kept telling my wife. "We grew up with Mickey, he didn't. He's not going to like it." (Although this could've all just been an excuse to get out of that God-forsaken line.) Finally, after an eternity, we get there. It was about to happen.

We were next in line, and to be honest I think I was more excited than Justice. And contrary to my fears…he loved it! In the days that followed, he would continue to say at seemingly random times, "I want to see Mickey!"

Bedtime? "I want to see Mickey!"

Bathtime? "I want to see Mickey!"

"Good morning, Justice!" I would say.

"Good morning, Daddy. Can we go see Mickey?"

Just like that, in only a moment it happened - my favorite childhood character was now my son's favorite. All because he met him.

If Only Bethel Had an Address

If only Bethel had an address - I'd wait in that line, stroller or no stroller. If it meant that my son would meet the creator of Heaven and Earth, the beginning and the end, the love of my life? I'd wait.

Especially if it meant that the God of my childhood would become the God of his childhood. I'd wait. I don't care if it were thousands of miles from home, accessible only by boat and plane. I would drive, swim, and fly - whatever it took. Just point me in the right direction.

The Bible is full of "Bethels," places where divine encounters and introduction take place between God and Man. But where are they today? Show me. So I can take my youth group, my sons, and my generation to meet God. If I've done my job so far, you should be asking the same question.

"I'm convinced! I want them to meet God! What do I do now?" Awesome! I'm glad you're on board! And I pray you maintain that excitement. Because, I have some sobering information to share.

What can you do? Something, and *nothing*. Why nothing? Let's go back to the arranged marriage story in Chapter 1. While you have the power to pick the person you want your son or daughter to spend the rest of his or her life with, no power on Earth can force them to fall in love with that person. It's a somber reality - no matter how much we want this generation to love Jesus, we can't *make* them love Jesus.

I must emphasize here, that if I was just trying to sell books, it's at this point that I would fabricate some promise. Perhaps I would invent a few stories to validate a false "99% success rate," to keep you reading. If that was the case, I would never tell you this, and to be honest, I struggle with whether or not I should be so blunt. But I've been in youth ministry for too long, and have witnessed too many stories to say anything other than the truth.

"How can I get my son\daughter, student, friend to love Jesus?" You can't.

Because, love doesn't work like that.

To "force" is to go contrary to the design of love, because love is a choice. This is the beauty of free will - without it, we could never truly love God (a mystery we explore in Chapter 6). They have to decide on their own whether or not God is someone they want to spend the rest of their lives with.

"So, why am I reading this book?"

Well, to reverse a popular maxim, "You can't force a horse to drink, but you can lead it to the water."

You can take this generation to Bethel, or better said, build it. You see, Bethel isn't a particular place. It's not your church, home, or youth conference. Though before Jesus, it was. Before Jesus, Jerusalem was the Bethel of the people. If you wanted to meet God, you had to pack your bags, prepare food portions, and travel to the Temple - at least once a year. But, when Jesus died on the cross, something special happened.

At the moment of his death, the Bible tells us that "the veil" in the Temple (the curtain that hid God's presence) was torn. This veil was a symbolic barrier between God and humanity. And through Christ, that barrier is now broken. This was a sign that the presence of God would no longer be limited to a particular location or building. Now, the Holy Spirit would reside in man. Each man would now become God's own temple.

Until this tearing of the veil, the revelation of the Lord was limited to the Hebrew people and those around them. But the stage was now set for the great introduction between God and the rest of humanity. This is the Easter message summarized in 6 words:

The world can now meet God.

Bethel has no address, and that's a good thing. Because Bethel - translated the "house of God" - is wherever God lives. Our job is simple: to create environments at home and at church, that invite God to move in. Bethel has evolved. It's no longer a place…but a process.

The Process of Creating Environments

One of Israel's greatest accomplishments was the building of Solomon's Temple. Aside from its beauty and splendor, what really set it apart, was that it became a dwelling place for God on Earth; a dwelling where His presence would reside. It's important to note however, that God doesn't move in the moment the door is put on the hinges. Even though Solomon followed the Heavenly blueprints to code, and each inch measured to perfection, the construction was not complete.

Following the construction came a process: a dedication, a sacrifice, but most notably, a prayer. A prayer so powerful, that an environment was created, and God moved in.

"But will God really dwell on earth with humans? The heavens, even the highest heavens, cannot contain you. How much less this temple I have built…Now arise, Lord God, and come to your resting place, you and the ark of your might." 2 Chronicles 6:18, 41

Now look at what happens immediately after Solomon says "Amen":

"When Solomon finished praying, fire came down from heaven and consumed the burnt offering and the sacrifices, and the glory of the Lord filled the temple." 2 Chronicles 7:1

It wasn't the building that Solomon built that drew God, but rather the environment he created that invited God's glory. As leaders, this is our responsibility. It's not only all we can do, it's what we *must* do. We must create environments that invite God's presence for a generation to encounter. We have a big part - and at the same time no part - in their "Hello" moment with God. If this sounds a bit confusing, here's a great example in the natural world.

I do not work well with plants. To be honest, I've never given it a fair shot - I simply don't have the patience. My grandmother does though, and one thing she taught me was, "You can't make plants grow." Well, that was news to me. I mean, I saw her plant the seed; I saw her water the plant; I saw the plant grow. So, what do you mean you can't make a plant grow?

"The sun makes the plant grow," she replied. "All I do is create an environment."

That makes sense, and I think it has truth for parents, leaders, and pastors. We can't force this generation to grow or to love, but what we can do is create environments, through a process, where they can meet Him. I hope to share this process with you in the upcoming chapters, but I also offer a word of caution.

Caution: None of this works without…

This is not a formula.

There is no formula.

You can love this generation a lot, and love Jesus a lot, but what we're about to discuss will rest on one vital virtue. Without this, all your efforts will come to nothing.

That virtue is: *patience.*

Like the line at Disney I had to wait in, or the farmer who faithfully waters an invisible seed buried beneath the dirt for weeks before he sees any sign of life, the ultimate virtue a leader or parent can have with this generation is patience. In the end, there is this humble and sobering acceptance that God is God, and He works in His own time. That's the bad news, if you could call it that. He's the only one who has the power to step out of Heaven.

Here's the good news: He stepped out of Heaven once before, and He can do it again. No one loves this generation more than Him. His Holy Spirit is ready to move in to any living temple that invites him. Preparing the environment is our part, then waiting for God to do His part.

Bethel's Building Blocks: Intimacy, the Supernatural, and Vocation

After gathering the many "Hello" moments in Scripture, I couldn't help but notice that there was a common thread woven through each encounter. Three elements in particular seemed to dominate the narratives. Every meeting was:

Intimate

Supernatural

Vocational

That begged the question - how do leaders, parents, and pastors create environments where intimacy is born, the supernatural is experienced, and a vocation is conferred?

An Intimate Encounter: The Gospel

The first thing that stands out is the personal transformation each person experiences before and after encountering God's presence. Moses went from a shepherd/refugee/recluse to a man who talked with God face to face. Jacob turned into Israel, a man who wrestled with God. Saul began trying to wipe the world of Christ, then turned into Paul who would willingly die in order to know Christ (Philippians 3:10). And just read Acts 2:42–47 to see the kind of men and women the people in that upper room became.

What led to their transformations? In each case, it was a lifestyle of prayer and devotion. An intimacy forged from the fires of their encounter. It was love at first sight when these men and women met God. They would never be the same again. Intimacy precedes devotion; it's the driving force behind encounter.

So, how do we create an environment that nurtures romance between God and a generation?

By sharing the greatest love story ever told: the Gospel.

A Gospel told best when empowered by the Holy Spirit.

A Supernatural Encounter: The Holy Spirit

A burning bush, a heavenly ladder, a blinding light, tongues of fire - God knows how to make an impression! But there's more to this approach than just signs and wonders. God's not in the business of "impressing." We prove ourselves to Him, not the other way around. The supernatural is often misunderstood as the "flexing of God's biceps." And while it can be that at times - visually impressive and powerful - supernatural experience is not limited to that.

Just revisit the story of God and Elijah at Horeb (1 Kings, chapter 19). God chooses to introduce himself there, not in an earthquake or fire, but rather, in a whisper.

"Go out and stand before me on the mountain," the Lord told him. And as Elijah stood there, the Lord passed by, and a mighty windstorm hit the mountain. It was such a terrible blast that the rocks were torn loose, but the Lord was not in the wind. After the wind there was an earthquake, but the Lord was not in the earthquake. And after the earthquake there was a fire, but the Lord was not in the fire. And after the fire there was the sound of a gentle whisper. When Elijah heard it, he wrapped his face in his cloak and went out and stood at the entrance of the cave. And a voice said, "What are you doing here, Elijah?" (1 Kings 19:11–13 NLT)

It's safe to say that was no ordinary whisper. It's safe to say that was a supernatural whisper. What made it supernatural? Simple: it couldn't be discerned by the 5 natural senses. It spoke not to his rationale or reason, but to his inner man. He didn't just hear the whisper with his ears, he heard it with his Spirit, supernaturally, in a way only God can.

How do we create environments where the supernatural is welcome? We talk about, invite, wait, then listen for the Holy Spirit.

When the Spirit grabs hold of your heart, you end up like Peter on the Day of Pentecost, unable to contain the "fire in his bones" (Jeremiah 20:9). You become missional.

A Vocational Encounter: Their Mission

What do Moses, Jacob, Paul, and the 120 people gathered in the upper room in Acts chapter 2 have in common? They all met God, and they all left that meeting with a mission.

Every encounter with God leads to a realization that you are part of a far bigger picture. When we meet God, He doesn't only become the love of our lives, but also the Lord of our lives. His glory requires our surrender, our weeping in humility. "Here I am Lord. Lead me. I'll follow."

How do we create environments where vocation is discovered? By sharing the mission.

Building Bethel requires leaders, parents, and pastors to:

Share the Gospel.

Invite the Holy Spirit.

Discover their Mission.

Let's start with the Gospel.

Have you ever shared the Gospel before with your students, children, or friends? Did you share the *whole thing*?

Chapter 6

I'M DYING TO MEET YOU

"So it's not gonna be easy. It's gonna be really hard. We're gonna have to work at this, every day, but I want to do that because I want you. I want all of you, forever, you and me, every day..."

—"Noah", The Notebook

Remember when we talked about the power of story in Chapter 3? About how important it is for this generation to develop their own, instead of living off the stories of their fathers? Well therein lies the challenge. What if they have no story? Where do we begin then? My story won't work. Neither will yours. It has to be theirs, but they don't have one.

Or do they?

It Was Us...

Have you ever seen or read *The Notebook*? It's a total "chick flick," and I hate that I love it. I can't watch it without my eyes watering. (Spoiler Alert) It is mine and my wife's personal goal to die in each other's arms, like the two main characters. But it has a great message.

The movie opens up with a scene of an older man and woman, somewhere in their sixties or seventies. To the woman, this man is a stranger; she's never seen him before in her life. It's clear from the dialogue, however, that the man knows her. He leads the woman to a nearby field where they sit down, and he pulls out a notebook. He begins to read her a story. It's a great story, about a great love - a love that was perfect, then lost, then saved.

The woman is captivated. She loves the story. But as she continues to hear it, something happens. Something inside of her awakens; something dormant and forgotten, but not dead. She begins to feel the love within the story - not as an observer - but as a participator, as if she was *in* the story.

Then, in a flash, she remembers that this story is not someone else's story - this is *her* story. And this man who she thought was a stranger, he was no stranger. He's her husband, the love of her life. Great stories have the power to awaken things inside of you, things you didn't even know were there…about yourself.

"I remember now," the main character begins to weep. *"It was us."*

An amazing thing happens when a young person hears the greatest love story ever told. The story about a God who gave up his throne and became a man, to save all men. They begin to realize that this isn't someone else's story, this is their story. And the God who's telling it to them, He's no stranger; He's the love of their life.

The first step in bringing a generation to know God is bringing them to know God's story of love. You can't know God without knowing His love. That's the difference between an atheist academic with a Ph.D. in religion and a 7-year-old boy who prays every night. Which one knows God? The person who knows that He loves him. The more you know His love, the more you know Him.

How does someone get to know God's love?

Ask someone who knows it.

Someone like John…the *Beloved.*

The Beloved

There were 12 people on this earth who knew God like few of us ever will. They saw Him, ate with Him, cried with Him, laughed with Him, hugged Him, felt His beard against their cheeks, watched Him die, and witnessed when He came back to life. For three years, they spent almost every waking moment with Him. Of these 12 who knew Him well, it can be argued that John knew Him best.

When the rest of the disciples were sent away so that Jesus could have some privacy, John was one of the three that stayed. He was V.I.P. Of the three disciples who got to see what the others could not, only John could be caught "reclining against him." When Jesus had a secret that someone really wanted to know, only John could get it out of him (John 13:24). Jesus and John were so close that John was the only one the Lord confided in to receive and spread the news of what would take place at the end of times — what would become known as the book of Revelations. John was the one Jesus gave that knowledge to.

Though for anyone familiar with John's story, this really isn't a surprise, not when his nickname was: "The one that Jesus loves." John's relationship with Jesus gave him insight into who God really was. I call it the "Louis Lane Effect," after the Superman comics. The whole world knew who Superman was, all 7 billion. But only one person knew who he really was — Louis Lane. Why? Because Superman loved her so much, he revealed his true identity (Clark Kent) to her.

Similarly, John's relationship allowed him to peer into the

depths of God, and John revealed His true identity to the rest of the world:

"God is love." - 1 John 4:8

God is love. That's not information, that's revelation. What's the difference? Information is something you learn; revelation is something you realize. REAL-ize — as in, it becomes real.

One day, something supernatural happens in the life of a young person: the sentence "Jesus loves me," which is information kids hear all their lives, evolves into something beautifully new and infinitely better: "Jesus loves *me.*"

As a pastor and parent, I can tell you that's the greatest revelation you can ever hope for your students and children to have. And, you can help them have it.

How?

How does one help a young person arrive at this revelation? Well I've got good news and bad news. To be specific, one piece of bad news, and two pieces of good news.

The bad news is (I suggest always starting with the bad news): only God can do it. 1 Corinthians 12:3 says, "No one can say Jesus is Lord, except by the Holy Spirit." Information comes from man, but revelation comes from God.

On to the good news. The good news is:

Good News #1: God *wants* this generation to know He loves them more than anyone, because "He is not wishing for any to perish, but for all to come to repentance." - 2 Peter 3:8–10

Good News #2: The revelation *is* the "Good News." God's love is revealed through something we already have: the Gospel.

"God showed how much he loved us by sending his one and only Son into the world so that we might have eternal life through him. This is real love—not that we loved God, but that he loved us and sent his Son as a sacrifice to take away our sins. - 1 John 4:9–10"

The greatest revelation of God's love is the Gospel, which literally means "the good news." Then, why don't more people love God? Surely in my church, as in your church, everyone's heard the Gospel, right?

Do You "Get" the Gospel?

"I get it. I finally get it." That was what she said.

It was the last Youth service before Easter Sunday. Around this time, our Youth group typically takes a break from our scheduled sermon series to preach the Easter message. I must shamefully admit that, at that time, I was a bit lethargic in my sermon prep. It's not that I don't love Easter - Easter is the message our faith was built on. It's just that...you have to work really hard to preach something well that you know everyone's heard a million times Because, you know, the story never changes.

David beats Goliath. He always does.

Moses gets to the Red Sea, and it splits. It always does.

Jesus dies on the cross, and He comes back to life. He always does.

You can't really get creative with the story. That's called heresy.

It's so easy though, isn't it? To skip or fast-forward through the "simple" things about God? It's almost as if there's this subconscious pressure to pull out the "deep things." After all, anything worth learning takes work. There are some stories that are told so often, we as parents or teachers feel like we have to really dig into them in order to extract value. But here's what I learned about the Gospel that Wednesday night:

You don't have to dig into the Gospel to find value. *The Gospel story digs into us...and finds value.*

I'm so glad that night I decided to simply preach the Gospel, because something special happened. By the end of the sermon, hundreds of students were at the altar weeping and meditating on the person of Christ and what He had done for them. Usually, Easter messages were a time when our students gave thanks. This was different. This was repentance. They met God.

One girl in particular really caught my attention. On my way off the stage, she grabbed me, tears streaming down her face, and said the words I will never forget; words that have made me excited to preach the Gospel ever since:

"I get it. I finally get it."

She went on to tell me how she's heard about Jesus and the cross her whole life, but never really understood what Christ had done. I figured maybe this girl was new to church, or maybe her parents were. But then that Sunday I got to preach the same message to our adult congregation. It had the same result. And while making my way back to my seat, I was approached again. This time by a man who appeared to be in his 40s. Much older than the girl at youth service, but looking just as desperate and relieved as she had. He said to me, "I'm 43 years old. My father's a Pastor in New York. I grew up in church my whole life. And this is the first time I understand what Jesus did for me on the cross."

I couldn't decide if I should be happy or sad. How do you go through church your whole life, and just now "get" it? That was when I realized that there's not only a difference between knowing about God, and knowing God, but *there's also a difference between knowing about the story and knowing the story.* The worst assumption we teachers and parents could ever make about our students and children is to assume that because they've grown up in church, they know the Gospel.

So what made the difference in the sermon you ask? What video clip did I use? What drama did I do? What object lesson did I bring? None. I did nothing special, except that, for the first time, I preached the whole story.

The Whole Gospel

I learned that Matthew, Mark, Luke, and John were not the only books in the Bible that talked about Jesus - that they weren't the only books that preached the Gospel. At least, not the whole Gospel. I realized in preaching to unchurched students, and really even to the students who've grown up in church, that the reason why they have trouble "getting" it, is because we try to make the middle of the story the whole story.

"Jesus was born, lived a perfect life, died on a cross for you and me, then rose again, so that we would could live forever."

But that's not the Gospel, at least, not all of it. In churches and homes, that is often the incomplete version that's taught: a gospel that centers around the fact that we are sinners in need of a savior. However, the Gospel is a story, not a statement.

I told the whole story, and here is that story, in a simple way, that you can share with your friends, children, students, or church.

The whole Gospel has 4 parts: Creation, the Fall, Redemption, and Restoration.

Chapter 7

THE GOSPEL IS A STORY ...NOT A STATEMENT

The Gospel is a love story, not a formula.

– Donald Miller

Statements alienate people. As soon as they're made, you're either for it or against it. This is a part of the reason why Jesus taught more stories than made statements. You don't "get" statements; you either agree, or disagree with them. Allow me to demonstrate:

"Jesus loves you." (statement)

"Jesus died for your sins." (statement)

"Jesus is the only way to Heaven." (statement)

I agree with them all. But your kids might not. In fact, there's a good chance they won't. Why? Because, this postmodern generation hates statements. They don't process truth through absolutes. No shocking news here. They hate being told what to do, what's right, and what's wrong.

They process truth through stories. As teachers, we allow them to interpret the story - to wrestle with the characters and the plot, to examine the problem and find the solution. In that process revelation is born. The Holy Spirit illuminates their understanding, and finally, the listener gets it. If we limit the Gospel to a message of redemption by only focusing on "Jesus died for your sins," then we're not telling a story - we're making a statement. This generation will reject it.

We need to preach the Gospel by telling the story of the relationship between God and Man, while remembering that intimacy is the driving force behind an encounter. This is our story, your story, my story, your student's story, your son and daughter's story - and it starts in the beginning.

The Gospel starts in Genesis.

Creation: God Made You For Relationship

For the most part, whenever we begin to teach the gospel we begin in Matthew. In that way, we're already cutting the story short. This is our first step: Creation.

When God created Adam, and you, and your children or students, it was not to torture them or to employ a massive work force. God doesn't need help doing anything; He's God. So, why did God create us? Good question. I don't know. Why do people have kids?

You ever think about that? I have two. Why did I do that? Do you know how expensive having kids is? Five-figures! Four, even after insurance! Not only that, but the moment they're born, kids are only good at three things: crying, eating, and pooping. Sometimes they will perform all three on *you*. Guess who has to feed, soothe, and clean them, at 3:15am? You! The parent. And for what? They've never done anything for you. All they've done since the moment they were born, and all they will continue to do for years to come, is take from you. Why would anyone in the world want kids? Good question. I don't know.

All I know is that from the moment I saw Justice, from the moment I held him, I felt a love like I've never felt before. I can't explain it. Parents know what I'm talking about. It's truly indescribable, and I couldn't figure out why. I was in awe, and at the same time confused about why I was in awe. Then my wife spoke, and I was stopped in my tracks, as if the Holy Spirit was speaking right through her.

She said, "Look at him. He looks just like you".

Wow. I couldn't process it in all the excitement and fear of the birthing process, but maybe one of the reasons why I loved him so much was because he looked like me. I don't mean just in physical appearance, but on the inside. His DNA, his blood was mine. He was a copy of me. I made him. And that was when it clicked,

"Then God said, 'Let us make mankind in our image, *in our likeness*. So God created mankind in his own image, in the image of God he created them; male and female he made them." - Genesis 1:26–27

You see, you have to start the story at Genesis, because Genesis is "the why" of the Gospel. It tells "why" God made us. It's the reason why God left Heaven for us. It's the "why" God died for us. Why? Because, you are literally a child of God. God loves you because He made you, and unlike any other creation in existence, He made you in His image. You look like Him.

And I can tell you as a dad that you never stop loving your kids. Never. Not when they cry, not when they've pooped, not when they're bad, not even when they run away.

Especially not when they run away. I know this because we ran, and God came running after.

The Fall: We Chose Another Relationship

God's love was perfect, our relationship with Him was perfect. But one day, we decided that God's love wasn't enough, that we wanted more. How do I know that? The same way God did; because of the tree in the garden. That stupid tree. God gave one rule: don't eat from the tree. Simple enough? It is, until you take into account the location of the tree.

Where was it planted? Right in the middle of the garden! What's the deal with that, God? That makes no sense. I have a son who loves cookies. Whenever my wife makes them, she makes sure to put them way in the corner of the kitchen, somewhere high. Why? As the saying goes, "Out of sight, out of mind." But putting the tree in the middle of the garden, and then telling Adam and Eve not to eat from it would be like me putting the cookies on a golden platter in the middle of my living room, with Christmas lights wrapped around the table, then expecting my son not to eat those cookies. That would be foolish. So then, what does that say about God? We know that "foolish" is never in the same sentence as God, unless He's talking about us. Then, why does He put the tree in the middle of the garden? Once again, John the Beloved has the answer.

The proof that we love God comes when we keep his commandments. (1 John 5:3)

Imagine for a moment that you and your spouse were the last two people on earth. You've survived the Zombie apocalypse (or Ape apocalypse depending on your sci-fi preferences), and now it's only you and her.

And moved by her spectacular awesomeness, you look deep into her eyes and say, "Baby, you're the most beautiful girl in the world." Would that touch her? Would it bring her to tears? Would it stir the depths of her soul? Probably not.

Because she's the *only* girl in the world! The comment means nothing. It falls flat. Why?

Because there are no other options.

This explains the tree and its placement. God wanted your love for Him to be genuine, and genuineness only comes through choice. He put the tree in the middle of the Garden so that Adam and Eve could see it from anywhere. Because, every time they saw it, and chose not to give in, it was like blowing God a kiss. Every time they kept walking, they were telling the Lord, "I love you more."

But one day, they chose differently. Although God's love was all they needed, for a second they were convinced that it wasn't all they wanted. When they chose against God, they chose for sin. And sin put a wedge between God and man, a gap. What do I mean by a "gap?" Imagine the space between the two opposite sides of the Grand Canyon. That gap – the Grand Canyon itself - is what sin became, that's what it is. You on one side, and God on the other.

Now it's important to remember that even in this position, God is not angry. He's desperate to get to you. That's why his first words after the Fall weren't, "I can't believe you did that!", or "How could you betray me!", or "You ingrate! A whole garden wasn't enough for you?" No. His first words were, *"Where are you?"* (Genesis 3:9).

You see, even from the other side of the canyon, He never stops loving you, He never stops desiring you. There's just this impassable chasm, called sin. And, because sin and God are incompatible, there's no way He can get to you. It's like oil in water; all they do is separate. God is so holy, that they can never touch.

So what does He do? He creates a "sin band-aid," a temporary solution for the problem of sin. When He finds Adam and Eve hiding behind a bush, the Bible says "The Lord God made garments of skin for Adam and his wife and *covered* them" (Genesis 3:21). Let me tell you, He didn't buy those animal garments at the mall. He killed the animal, and with its bloody skin, wrapped humanity. The animal died, and its blood was spilled - life for life. This is when the practice of sacrifice was born.

But, these animal skins were just band-aids. They could "cover" sin like deodorant does stench, but mankind didn't need a deodorant, they needed a bath. They needed to remove sin so that God could get close again. He doesn't just want to live *with* us, he wants to live *in* us. That's why the final plan was to *remove* sin, not just hide it. Animals couldn't do that. Listen to what the Bible says,

"It is impossible for the blood of bulls and goats to take away sins" (Hebrews 10:4).

So what will we do? How will God ever get to us? How will sin ever be removed? Just keep reading the verse:

"That is why Christ came into the world" (Hebrews 10:5).

Redemption: He fixes the Relationship

Jesus was the perfect sacrifice, the sacrifice to remove sin "once and for all" (Hebrews 10:10). Only Jesus could do it, and here's three reasons why:

1. The sacrifice had to be perfect

The sacrifice had to be perfect, which means blameless, never having done wrong. That is why animal sacrifices worked temporarily. The animals were innocent and blameless. But they couldn't fulfill requirement #2.

2. The sacrifice had to be a Man.

The Scriptures tell us, "The first man, Adam, became a living person. But the last Adam — that is, Christ — is a life-giving Spirit" (1 Corinthians 15:45). If sin came into this world through a man, it would have to leave through a man. Therein lies the problem: men come in different shapes, sizes, and colors. You can find big ones, little ones, light ones, dark ones, but one kind you'll never find is a perfect one (and all the ladies said "Amen!"). We needed a Perfect-Man. But no man is perfect. There's no way out.

How will we be saved? We're all doomed. Only God is perfect.

If only there was some…"God-Man;" a combination of perfection and humanity. But that's ludicrous. "God-Man"? Who's ever heard of such a thing? Oh wait, Jesus! The Bible says, "The Word was God, and the Word became Man" (John 1). It could only be Jesus. Every religion in the world teaches in some way, shape, or form how a man can get to God. But, we're too flawed as individuals. God knew we'd never make it, so instead, He came to us! This brings us to the final and most improbable requirement.

3. The sacrifice has to choose.

We, chose to sin. Therefore, the sacrifice would have to choose to die in our place. This is perhaps the most impossible of the three. I can imagine a blameless God, even a God-Man, but I can't imagine that God-Man choosing to lay down his life, for me.

This was the greatest flaw in the practice of animal sacrifice. Every goat, bull, and lamb that was ever sacrificed on the altar was dragged there. They were pulled and pushed into place, frantic and panicked, struggling to escape. But, not Jesus. He wasn't forced to Calvary — He carried His cross. He said, "No one can take my life from me. I sacrifice it voluntarily" (John 10:18).

The goat screamed for its life as the knife pierced into its flesh. Here's what Jesus said when the nails were pierced into his: "Father forgive them. For they know not what they do." Hallelujah! Sin has been removed.

Restoration: We're Working On The Relationship

But the story doesn't end there. This is an important note, because if we end the story at salvation, then your student's story ends at salvation. In other words, once they say the prayer, they're done. Traditionally, this is where the Gospel ends. But, it's really just the beginning. Now begins the process of restoration, in us and in the World.

Continuing the story into the process of restoration is critical. If we end the story at the cross, then we leave this generation of followers as a group of frustrated young Christians, wondering why they're still struggling with their old selves, when they're supposed to be "saved." Hasn't sin been removed? Then why do they still do it? It's because meeting God is just the beginning. Now, His Spirit begins to work on our character, weaknesses, fears, and lives. This is some of the best news a young person can hear: We are each a work in progress. We are all in a process of restoration. We make mistakes and slip, but that's ok, because God is working in us as we work on the relationship.

Restoration gives this generation of believers what they sorely lack: hope. The hope that God isn't done with them. That the condition they're in is not their final state. God is restoring them, every day, to look more and more like Jesus. And one day, He'll restore them completely.

Restoration also gives this generation something else they desire: a mission. When you understand that you're not currently in the state that God intended, you also understand that this world is not in the state that God intended. Homelessness, poverty, sex trafficking, and mass shootings - the world is broken. It needs to be restored. And that's the most exciting part of the story! *We* are the restorers! God is not only working *in* us, but he's also working *through* us. Little by little, with every child fed, and every disease eradicated, the world is being restored. Until one day, when Jesus comes back and puts on the final touches. He will restore the world to what it was like in the beginning, restore us to what we were like in the beginning, and restore our relationship with God to what it was like in the beginning.

I have a Christian t-shirt in my closet that I think represents this generation so well. It's an image of a couple of stick figures. One is a young person, and the other a pastor. You can tell from the image that the pastor is upset at the young person for being distracted during his preaching. Above the teen's face it says, "I don't have ADD, I'm just bored."

What happens when we leave restoration out of the story? We have a church full of bored teenagers. A generation that can't wait for service to be over so they can get out and do something. The gospel story says that God has given them something to do, something great. It says that they have a calling on this earth, a mission to restore.

The story doesn't end at the resurrection. It's just getting started. As we see, the most exciting part is yet to be written.

VASQUEZ

Chapter 8

GHOST STORIES

There is no better evangelist in the world
than the Holy Spirit.

~ D.L Moody

The Gospel is a story, yet so much more. It isn't the late night "Once upon a time" type of story that we tell our kids so they sleep well. It's a disruptive, empire-shaking, society-shifting "For a time like this, you were born" type of story. It's not designed to put you to sleep, but to wake you up.

Over the course of history, this story has been told in many ways. First in letters, then in sermons, in the images of stained glass windows, songs, and most currently in film. Interestingly enough, the effectiveness of the message has not changed with the medium, because the effectiveness doesn't depend on the medium. What makes a story is never the paper it's written on, or the font that's used for the words - these things change depending on what the audience relates to better. What makes a story effective is the same thing that makes a joke effective - *the one who tells it.*

Every group of friends has the "go-to" storyteller - you know the one. The person everybody turns to and says, "No! You tell it! You tell it better!" Even if the whole group has heard it before, and all shares the same facts, there's something about the way that one person tells it that makes you feel like you were there. You're connected to the narrative.

Similarly, within the trinity of God lies the greatest storyteller of all time. He's the key to seeing this story bear fruit in the next generation. It will not be by people's skill or relevancy, our imagery or humor. "Not by might, nor by power — but by my Spirit, says the Lord" (Zechariah 4:6). Not by the eloquence of a man, not by good music, not by good preaching, but it is by the Spirit that God works His mighty work.

He Was There

When we make room for the Holy Spirit, we're making room for the greatest storyteller of all time. He's been telling stories for millennia, and continues to speak today. If we really want this story to stick, engage, and transform the next generation of followers - we better let Him tell it. He's been doing it for years. Moses wrote the book of Genesis, but he didn't tell the story. He wasn't there; he had no first hand knowledge. The Holy Spirit told the story.

"For prophecy never had its origin in the human will, but prophets, though human, spoke from God *as they were carried along by the Holy Spirit.*" 2 Peter 1:21

Have you ever listened to someone try and tell a story about an experience that they never experienced? An accident they didn't witness, a prank they didn't participate in, someone else's borrowed memory? It usually falls flat. No one laughs, no one's engaged. Most of the time, the story is met with a sympathetic "I guess you had to be there." So true. Because the story will always be told best by the people who were actually there — and the Spirit was.

When the first foundations of the Earth were laid, "The Spirit of God was hovering over the surface of the waters" (Genesis 1:2). When Paul taught about a Jesus who was the Son of God - perfect, crucified, resurrected, and ascended, how did he do it? He never knew him on Earth. "This is what we speak, not in words taught us by human wisdom but in words taught by the Spirit, expressing spiritual truths in spiritual words" (1 Corinthians 2:13).

Indeed, it wasn't just Paul or Moses who received every word from the Spirit, but every God-sent prophet, pastor, and preacher who came after. It's an illusion that the Bible was written by men. It was no more written by a man than a book is written by a pen. The man was merely a tool in the hands of the storyteller, the Holy Spirit. That's what makes the word, "sharper than a double-edged sword, cutting between soul and spirit, between joint and marrow" (Hebrews 4:12). The Spirit was there. When He tells the story, He does it in a such a supernatural way that He brings you into it, so you transition from being a listener to a participator, and then hopefully, a contributor.

He Is Here

The Gospel story is powerful when we invite and allow the Holy Spirit to tell it. He tells it better. He always has. It's tempting in our sermon prep, or lessons with our kids to focus on humor, illustrations, fun, or structure. These things are helpful, but our words will only reach their ears. When we acknowledge, invite, and allow the Holy Spirit to tell the story through us, lives are changed, not just because He was "there," but because He is also *"here."* He is present, in the most intimate way imaginable.

Charles Spurgeon illustrates our dependency on the Spirit in sharing the Gospel story in his sermon, *The Power of the Holy Ghost.*

The Holy Ghost has a power over men's hearts. Now, men's hearts are very hard to affect. If you want to get at them for any worldly object, you can do it. A cheating world can win man's heart; a little gold can win man's heart; a trump of fame and a little clamor of applause can win man's heart. But there is not a minister breathing that can win man's heart himself. He can win his ears and make them listen; he can win his eyes, and fix those eyes upon him; he can win the attention, but the heart is very slippery. Yes! The heart is a fish that troubles all gospel fishermen to hold. You may sometimes pull it almost all out of the water; but, slimy as an eel, it slippeth between your fingers, and you have not captured it after all. Many a man has fancied that he has caught the heart, but has been disappointed. It would take a strong hunter to overtake the heart on the mountains. It is too fleet for human foot to approach. The Spirit alone has power over man's heart. Did you ever try your power on a heart? If any man thinks that a minister can convert the soul, I wish he would try…We cannot reach the soul, but the Holy Spirit can. Why, to me, there is some hope for some of you. I cannot save you; I cannot get at you. I make you cry sometimes— you wipe your eyes, and it is all over. But I know my Master can. That is my consolation. This power can save you as well as anybody else. It is able to break your heart, though it is an iron one; to make your eyes run with tears, though they have been like rocks before. His power is able this morning, if he will, to change your heart, to turn the current of all your ideas; to make you at once a child of God, to justify you in Christ. There is power enough in the Holy Spirit.

The world's greatest orators could not have done what Peter did that day of Pentecost. He convinced a group of Jews that their Messiah had come, that they had killed him, that he resurrected from the dead, then ascended to heaven, and was coming back. Ridiculous! Nonsense! Crazy! And the only thing crazier - is that 3,000 people believed him.

They believed him not because he made great points, but because for the first time in human history the Spirit of God was able to speak directly to man. The Comforter had come, and He did not have to try and grab hold of the "slippery hearts." Like a harpoon, the Spirit pierced right through.

"Now when they heard this, they were *pierced* to the heart, and said to Peter and the rest of the apostles: "Brethren, what shall we do?" (Acts 2:37).

"Pierced" to the heart. The English translation of the word here robs you from grasping the full power of what the Holy Spirit was doing in the hearers. In John 19:34, we also see the word "pierce":

"But one of the soldiers *pierced* His side with a spear, and immediately blood and water came out." John 19:34

In English they're the same word, but in its original language of Greek, they're not. The Greek word for pierce in John is *"nusso."* It means to stick in and pull out. The soldier stabbed Jesus, but then the spear withdrew. In Acts, the word for pierce is "KATAnusso". The word KATA is a preposition that means "straight through." It's the difference between being stabbed, and being shot with a bullet that goes through. In other words, the Holy Spirit had come down on the hearts of the hearers from Heaven, and penetrated the entire heart of man, through his defenses, through his logic, through his resistance, through his walls, and into his soul. That's what the Spirit does.

D. L. Moody once told the story to his student R.A. Torrey

about the day he met the Holy Spirit. He was a tremendous debater, a real stickler for logic and arguments. His method of preaching was to "try to reason with people, beg them and coax them to come [to Jesus]." But one day he ran into an elderly lady named "Auntie Cook." The lady told Moody that she was praying for him. He asked "Praying for what?" She said, "That you might get the power - the baptism of the Holy Spirit." One day on the streets of New York, without warning, he said the Holy Spirit came on him in such a powerful way that he crawled up an alley and raised his hand and prayed, "Oh God, stay your power, or I'll die." Then he said, "I went out from there preaching the same sermons with the same texts but oh, *the difference now.*"

Did God Really Say?

It's subtle, but true. Adam and Eve are standing at the Tree of the Knowledge of Good and Evil, when Satan slithers out from the branches and asks, "Did God really say you couldn't eat from any tree in the garden?" I don't know; did he? We never see any biblical evidence of God speaking to Eve. We know God spoke to Adam. But who told Eve?

Most likely it was Adam who, like every good parent or pastor, did his best to pass down "the rules." The only difference was that for Adam, they were more than rules: they were revelation, the words of God, *from* God. He heard God speak them to him. Eve, however, did not share in this moment, and as a result, she did not share in the revelation. These were not the words of God; these were the words of Adam. Same details, different source. She didn't have revelation; she had knowledge. A lot like our students today.

This generation needs to hear FROM God — not just a voice that shares what God said.

The Devil's not dumb. He could've approached Adam, but he chose the easier target. He knew that the daggers of his speech were no match for "the sword of the Spirit, which is the word of God" (Ephesians 6:17). When God speaks, the Devil loses, both in the World and in the heart of man.

We're in desperate need of the Storyteller. He's the one who convinces the world and makes the Gospel "click." Without him, church is a dry, outdated, and irrelevant social club. But with Him, the Bible is brought to life; our songs transcend melody and rhythm; our sermons become surgical instruments. He's the counselor, comforter, *and* communicator.

"And the Holy Spirit helps us in our weakness. For example, we don't know what God wants us to pray for. But the Holy Spirit prays for us with groanings that cannot be expressed in words." Romans 8:26 NLT

He speaks to us, through us, and on God's behalf. The key to a "Hello" moment with God, to hearing Him speak, is to understand *how* he speaks, which is through the Holy Spirit.

He is the "Hello" of God.

And often times, His greatest hurdle *is us*.

VASQUEZ

Chapter 9

WHEN GOD SHOWS UP

"Dear brothers and sisters, when I first came to you I
didn't use big words and brilliant ideas to try and
convince you of God's message. I just decided to
concentrate only on Jesus Christ and his death on the
cross. I came to you in weakness – timid and
trembling. I didn't try to convince you with wise and
persuasive words, <u>but you were convinced by a
demonstration of the Holy Spirit's power</u>, so that your
faith might not rest on what someone said, but on
God's power."

– 1 Corinthians 2:1–5

I woke up one morning to some bad ministry news. It was affecting me hard, and I was off to a bad day. My wife noticed my countenance and asked what was wrong. When I told her, she told me she knew what would make me feel better. She went up the stairs, grabbed something, and came back down. In her arms was Justice.

At the time, he was a baby, maybe 8 months or so. She placed him in my arms, and as I held him, he smiled. I can tell you that in that moment the burden of my day lifted. A peace rested on my soul, as if my son was the one holding me.

I was immediately comforted, but not by traditional means. Interestingly enough, he didn't offer me any advice or medication. He didn't try to make me laugh or cry. *He was just there.* It was his *presence,* and I knew I was going to be alright, that everything was going to be alright.

The Holy Spirit is defined as the "Parakletos": the comforter and counselor. In this word lies the secret to the way the Spirit speaks. "Parakletos" is a loaded Greek word, with pages of definitions, but that's probably the best picture of how He operates in our lives.

How do we get the Holy Spirit to tell the story? We don't. We invite Him to show up, to make His way down the stairs, and to rest on our children. Then, we allow His presence to do the communicating. He just has to show up.

Come Holy Spirit, Come

Before every youth service our team prays that God would "show up." What do we mean by this term? Is God hiding? Is he lost? Is he not here?

Well, in one sense, the Holy Spirit is already active and present in the lives of all humanity. God is omnipresent. He's everywhere. For believers, he's always present in His commitment to always stand by us, work for us, and turn everything for our good. "Behold, I am with you always, to the end of the age" (Matthew 28:20).

Even in the lives of people who are far from God, He's subtly working through family, adversity, and nature - prepping their hearts for an encounter. They don't understand him, but they feel Him. "And when He has come, He will convict the world of sin, and of righteousness, and of judgment: of sin, because they do not believe in Me" (John 16:8).

In addition, every time we choose to display kindness and mercy to those around us, God is present through us. "No one has ever seen God. But if we love each other, God lives in us, and his love is brought to full expression in us." (1 John 4:12)

But in another, supernatural sense, we see in Scripture that there are times where God's Spirit gathers himself powerfully into a place and moment in time. We see it rarely in the Old Testament, like at the dedication of Solomon's Temple (1 Kings 8). In the New Testament however, we see it more frequently, like on the day of Pentecost (Acts 2), in Cornelius' house (Acts 10), and when the believers gathered together to pray for courage (Acts 4).

This leads me to believe that now that the veil has been torn and God has "moved" to Earth, "showing up" is His expectation, and it should be ours too. When the Gospel is preached in this kind of atmosphere, one that welcomes the Holy Spirit, "Hello" moments are born.

Any Time, Any Place

In D.L. Moody's story, God showed up while he was walking down the street. I have a good friend who's pastoring a growing church in Washington, who tells the story of God showing up while she was on a plane. Humorously, she emphasizes, "While I was in the middle seat!"

Every time we try and put God in a box, He breaks it. His power and will cannot be limited. R.T. Kendall said, "The Holy Spirit has His own personality. He therefore moves in at will when we least expect it, and sometimes when we are least deserving of it." When you understand that the Holy Spirit is a person, you understand that He can show up at any time, at any place. While there's nothing we can do to restrain Him, there are things we can do to welcome Him.

Despite church language, you don't "get" the Holy Spirit. Because you don't "get" people; you get things. I didn't get my wife. I met my wife. When students encounter the Holy Spirit, they meet God, and an authentic relationship can begin. We set the atmosphere, and invite Him to enter.

Let me be clear. There's nothing we can do to make God love us more. But, there are things we can do to draw Him closer. God's love never changes. At our worst and at our best, God loves us all the same. Like my wife loves me all the same. Sometimes, I do things that make her want to leave the room - like leaving my clothes hanging from the kitchen chair - and at other times, I do things that make her want to hug me - like washing the dishes without being asked. Don't confuse God's love with God's presence. God loves the world, but His presence brings intimacy. God's love is free. There's a cost to intimacy - to getting close.

Paul said, "Do not stifle the Holy Spirit" (1 Thessalonians 5:19). "And do not bring sorrow to God's Holy Spirit by the way you live" (Ephesians 4:30). Jesus said, do not "blaspheme" the Holy Spirit. (Mark 3:29). The Bible is clear. There are things we can do that push God away. And there are also things we can do to bring God close: "Come close to God and He will come close to you" (James 4:8)

Hide and Seek

As a parent, I play it often with my children. I hide, they find me; but even then, the game isn't over. The second half of the game begins when he gets close. I say, "You can't get me!" Then my son begins the chase.

But stop and take a second to think about what this game must look like to someone who has never seen it played before. "Why don't you just let him catch you?" the onlooker shouts. "He wants a hug from his daddy! Stop torturing the kid!" But they're not seeing the game from the perspective of the father. How does *he* win? If he's caught, he loses. If he hides so well that he's never found, then he loses. That's because for the father, it's not about being caught, or even about hiding: it's about being pursued. It's the seeking that excites him.

"Now set your mind and heart to *seek* the Lord your God" (1 Chronicles 22:19). "If then you have been raised with Christ, *seek* the things that are above, where Christ is, seated at the right hand of God. Set your minds on things that are above, not on things that are on earth" (Colossians 3:1–2).

I love how John Piper describes this concept of "seeking":

There are seasons when we become neglectful of God and give him no thought and do not put trust in him and we find him "unmanifested" — that is, unperceived as great and beautiful and valuable by the eyes of our hearts...That is why we are told to "seek his presence continually."...But what does that mean practically?...It is the conscious fixing or focusing of our mind's attention and our heart's affection on God. This setting of the mind is the opposite of mental coasting. It is a conscious choice to direct the heart toward God...It is a conscious effort on our part...We do not make this mental and emotional effort to seek God because he is lost. That's why we would seek a coin or a sheep. But God is not lost. Nevertheless, there is always something through which or around which we must go to meet him consciously. This going through or around is what seeking is. He is often hidden. Veiled.

Seeking God is about focusing, blocking out distractions, fighting through apathy, and throwing yourself into a pursuit of God. It can be done through singing, fasting, praying, reading the Word, or simply obeying what the Word tells you. The prophet Elisha used to use music to help him:

"But now, get me a player of music, and it will come about that while the man is playing, the hand of the Lord will come on me and I will give you the word of the Lord: and they got a player of music, and while the man was playing, the hand of the Lord was on him." (2 Kings 3:15).

It wasn't so much the musician that brought the hand of the Lord on Elisha, but rather what the musician helped Elisha to do - to focus on God, to seek him.

Here's the catch though - students will rarely "jump" into this. They need to be led and inspired to seek. They need to see an example. We are that example, and as we move, they move. As they move, God moves. God's love is unconditional; He'll love you no matter what. But, His manifested Presence - *that's* conditional. The presence of God depends on you. "You will seek me and find me WHEN you search for me with all your heart." (Jeremiah 29:13) This is something both taught *and* caught.

Some things are Taught AND Caught

I used to hear it all the time growing up: "Some things are taught, and some things are caught." I often heard it at church. That's how my youth pastor would explain the difference between the kids who had their arms held high, engaged in the worship experience, and others who sat down and stared into space.

He was trying to say that things like passion and pursuit could only be "caught." You had to be around it and people who did it enough, and you would "catch it". But years went by, and some never did. That's because, while there are some things that are taught and some that are caught, there are also things that are both taught and caught. Passion is one of those things.

One night when I was a teenager, I stayed over at the house of one the "passionate" kids. We played video games, watched cartoons, and went to bed. But before we did, his dad led us in prayer - a passionate prayer. He was teaching his son, and me, how to pray and seek the Lord. We can't wait for some people to "catch" what it means to seek. We have to intentionally teach that, *by example.*

One of the most important things we do in our youth ministry are "lock-ins." Throw out what you think an all-nighter at church with teenagers must look like. This is our schedule: Worship, the Word, and Prayer. We have some fun mixed in it too, but that's just the garnish on the dish. We invite our core leaders (the ones who know how to pray) and have them lead the charge. They teach on the importance of prayer and seeking God's presence. Because they recognize that seeking is caught *and* taught — just like the Holy Spirit.

Holy Who?

"We have not even heard that there is a Holy Spirit" (Acts 19:2).

I'll never forget a camp I ministered at one summer. I had just finished preaching on the Holy Spirit, and thank God he showed up. But what stuck out the most was a brief conversation I had with a youth pastor after the service. She approached me, visibly touched by God and encouraged by the message. "Thanks for doing what you did. It took real *courage* to talk about the Holy Spirit like that." Wait, what? Courage?

C.T. Studd once said, "How little chance the Holy Ghost has nowadays. The churches and missionary societies have so bound Him in red tape that they practically ask Him to sit in a corner while they do the work themselves."

He's probably the most ignored and misunderstood person in the church. Admittedly, some members in the body of Christ have left scary examples, but in response to these extreme "bad experiences," some have gone in the extreme opposite direction. Some leaders are afraid to talk about the Holy Spirit, or to give Him a place in our pulpits and homes. They expect people to "catch" Him. As if He was some sort of cold you get simply by being near the host. But, the Holy Spirit is more than merely caught, because He is more than merely an experience. The Holy Sprit must also be taught, because He is a person who provides an experience. *The Holy Spirit will not show up, if we don't acknowledge Him.*

You might say, "But God is God! Surely he's not limited by what we do, or do not do. If He wants to move in the supernatural, He'll move. If He chooses to send his Holy Spirit, He'll send Him. How dare anyone limit God to man's actions?"

But would you say the same about salvation? Would you say that if He wants people to be saved, He'll send Jesus into the hearts of man too? Of course God wants people to be saved. That's why He sent Jesus to earth. *But His will is still filtered through our willingness.* God saves people, but no one gets saved if they are not willing to preach to people about the Jesus that He sent. Would we expect people to put their trust in Jesus, if all we preached was about God the Father? The Gospel is not the Gospel without Jesus. And it's not the Gospel without the Holy Spirit, either.

Don't get me wrong, you know how I feel about the power of the Gospel. There's no greater name given unto man than the name of Jesus. Everything starts with the Gospel. I'm only shining light on our hidden thoughts: that we could imagine a church that doesn't preach about the Holy Spirit. But, we would never call a church "Church" if they didn't preach about Jesus - that would be heresy.

But why the distinction? Isn't the trinity 3-in-1? Or is it "2+1"? Could it be, that in our hearts, the Spirit is just not on the same level as the Father and the Son? Maybe we believe that He's not God, but a "product" of God?

The Holy Spirit is at work in the world, with or without us. That's true. But no, that doesn't mean that He should be left to advocate for Himself. In order for this generation to meet God, they need to encounter His Holy Spirit, and we need to teach about Him, and how to seek His presence - *then, get out of the way.*

Make Room

Last year I had the privilege of preaching at a Youth Convention of over 2,700 students. I'll never forget that experience. Not because of what I did, but because of what I learned about the Holy Spirit through my friend and host who invited me.

I preached for 40 minutes, called the students to the altar to meet God, and God showed up. About half the room responded. I prayed for as many as I could (about 15 minutes of just laying hands and ministering to people). When I was done (keyword being "I"), I handed the microphone back to my host, who was a local pastor in Dallas. The following hour would be a lesson in making room for the Holy Spirit. He grabbed the mic, closed his eyes, and knelt on the floor. He didn't say a word. For 45 minutes he was silent. What do you suppose happened?

In many of our churches the awkwardness of silence would have been too much for the pastor to bear. Many of us leaders would've ended on the high note, called it a night, and sent the students to their hotel rooms. Not him. He was sensitive enough to realize that God wasn't done, and humble enough to realize there was nothing he could say or do to help (as if anything we say or do is what transforms people). He did nothing, and that was exactly what was needed. By the time he opened his mouth, the other half of the room had completely responded, made their way to the altar, and was either weeping or prostrate.

What was happening? In the silence, the Holy Spirit was wrestling with the other students who needed God. He was idiosyncratically dismantling the arguments and stubbornness of the people. Each life had their own reasons for not responding. Perhaps they thought, "I'm not good enough", "Been there, done that, no change", "What will they think of me?" But the Holy Spirit, like only He could, began to speak, and it pierced right through.

The saddest thing for me that night was the realization that if I was in charge, we would've missed it. The Pastor made room for the Holy Spirit to do what only He could. In our churches and in our homes, we must do the same. There were no sermons in the upper room on the day of Pentecost that we know of - only praying and waiting. Sometimes our services, prayer times, and worship is so structured that we leave no room for God to step into the particulars of our lives. Sometimes, churches talk about finances, mercy, forgiveness, and faith, then hope that some of it "lands" in the hearts of the hearers. But when the Spirit speaks, He speaks exactly what we need to hear, measured to the details of our situation.

Because He knows our pain.

He knows our problems.

And He also knows our purpose.

Chapter 10

S.A.D.D.

For centuries, these two strategies – telling God's story and enacting it – comprised the heart of Christian formation.

– Kenda Creasy Dean

The tale of two fundraisers:

I know a church that had a *good* idea for a missions fundraiser: a coffee house. It was meticulously planned and thought through. Engaging bands were invited, spoken words were shared, and the lights were dim. It was definitely a cool place to hang, and of course - for a great cause. It raised very little support.

I know another church that had a *dangerous* idea for a missions fundraiser: A Tough Mudder Race. It was also planed well. Barbwire was setup, ditches were dug, and obstacles were built. It raised tons of support. Why would someone pay to be tortured? They're not. They're paying to participate in a mission.

Jeff Fromm, an authority on marketing to the "millennial" generation said this, "[They] are intrigued by opportunities that offer a unique stamp of achievement, combined with a bit of recklessness, all for a 'cause outside myself.' It's not the 'me generation,' it's the 'me plus the world generation.'"

> When Moses met God at Horeb, he left that meeting with a mission.
>
> When Saul met God on the road to Damascus, he left that meeting with a mission.
>
> When the 120 described in Acts met God on the day of Pentecost, they left that meeting with a mission.

The authenticity of every encounter is sealed with a mission, or better put, a "vocation." This generation is in need of a calling. The world has been brought to their finger tips, and it only highlights how empty they are. How do you differentiate between an emotional experience and a God-experience? The God experience comes with vision, with vocation - internal challenges for your life, family, community, and world.

Every man is in search for a purpose. This is why every man ought to find God. When we find God, we find our purpose. No one knows how something works like the one who invented it, and every man was an invention dreamt up in the mind of God.

Ezekiel 36:26 says, "I will give you a new heart and put a new spirit in you; I will remove from you your heart of stone and give you a heart of flesh." You can't get a new spirit without getting a new heart — it's a package deal. And in that new heart, vocation lies. When the Spirit fills your life He brings with him a very special passion. He brings a passion that will forever serve as a compass for your purpose.

The Proof is in the Pudding <u>Passion</u>

I have a confession. One night after church, immediately after my sermon, I grabbed my wife and left for the car. Anybody in pastoral ministry knows that after the service is prime time. People want to talk with their Pastors, they want to ask questions and say hi. But, I was temporarily gripped by selfishness. We had to be home by 9pm. *Had to.* I'm almost ashamed to say why. It was to see the season's finale of one of our favorite shows.

But that's not the shameful part. What's shameful is the show I went home to watch - *Project Runway* (and there goes my man-card).

I don't know if you've ever seen it or not. But it's one of those reality shows where different fashion designers compete and are judged on their creative abilities to sew clothes. For some reason, I love to watch this with my wife. Recently, I figured out why. I have *zero* fashion sense. I hate shopping for clothes, I hate picking out the clothes we shopped, and I hate making sure that what you picked out "goes" together. I can't stand the process. If you ask me, (and the Bible) clothes are a curse; the result of the Fall; they're Adam and Eve's fault!

But my wife's a *fashionista*. She has great taste and thought seriously about pursuing a career in the fashion industry. As a result, her husband and children are always dressed well, and we have *nothing* to do with it. We are the product of her passion.

We also only have one TV in our house. Going off the recommendation of our pastor when we first got married: one TV forces the couple to sit down together and spend quality time, verses me watching my shows in one room and she watching hers in another. It's worked so far, so we just kept it that way.

Another byproduct of the one-TV rule has been practicing our communication and negotiation skills. With only one TV (and through the magic of DVR) my wife and I have to both agree on what we're going to watch that night. That means if a big playoff game is on that night, we're watching the playoffs. Unfortunately though, every night can't be playoffs (sigh), so on open nights we watch what she wants to watch: *Project Runway.* For the early years of our marriage, it took an Herculean effort to sit through a single episode. Because it wasn't enough to "just watch." I had to engage and ask questions, really attempt to be interested. Questions like, "What's *Avant-guard* mean?" or "What does it mean to be *chic?*"

After a while, the attempts to show my wife that I care became actual caring. It wasn't a struggle to sit down and watch a show with her. I actually wanted to do it. That's when I learned a valuable lesson: *When you love someone, their passions become your passions.* And can you guess what God is passionate about? You guessed right: People.

After a genuine, intimate encounter with God's Spirit, a slow but persistent transformation begins on the inside. It's like a heart transplant - one that takes years, and sometimes a lifetime, to finish (if ever finished). That heart of stone becomes a heart of flesh, and the heart of flesh is made sensitive by a love for God. It begins to beat for the things God's heart beats for.

Jesus summarized this phenomenon in the two greatest commandments: "The first and greatest commandment is Love the Lord your God, and the second is like it, love your neighbor" (Matthew 22:37-39). At first glance, many well-intentioned Bible students make the mistake that assuming the first commandment (Love God) is better or "all important," as if doing only that would compensate for not following the second commandment, the commandment to love your neighbor.

But notice that Jesus says, "And the second *is like it...*" The Greek word for "like" here is the same word that translates as "reflection." When I look in a mirror, I see an image of me. It's not me however. I am me. The image is *"like me."* The vocabulary here unlocks the true meaning of what Jesus is trying to say. To love your neighbor isn't less important than loving God. It *is* loving God; it's a reflection of loving God. *It's second in order, not in importance.* It's the natural response to seeing God, to loving him, it's what must follow.

The Heart of Vocation

Mark Twain said, "The two most important days in your life are the day you are born and the day you find out why." This dual passion for God and people is at the heart of vocation - it becomes the *"why"*, the greater purpose this generation is so desperately seeking. Once they have it, it becomes translated by the unique spiritual gifts, talents, and abilities they possess.

For some people that means asking the question, "How can I love God and people through my athletic achievements?" For others, through the academic world. Others with the medical, artistic, or ministerial worlds. Every person's "calling" is different, but we all have the same vocation.

In my experience working with young people, figuring out the "what" is often difficult for them. They ask, "What do I do with my life?" "What will be my career?" "What's my calling?" But half of that difficulty is handled once they realize they're asking the wrong question. Once they grab on to the "why," the "what" is like a liquid, forming to whatever shape the bottle is. The bottle is the "why"; the bottle is our vocation.

The "what" changes in every season of life, especially for students. One day, you're a child joining a Bible club in your school, the next day you're leading your high school team in prayer before the big game, the next day you're coaching your son's little league team. If we can lead students into an encounter with God, they begin discovering their vocation, their mission.

S.A.D.D.

No one in my family has ever been diagnosed with A.D.D. (Attention Deficit Disorder). Then again, no one in my family has bothered to get checked. My dad swears he has it, my sister has to have it it (you would agree if you met her), and you wouldn't believe the things that pass through my mind in church.

But with respect to those who really do suffer from this disorder, I once read a study that made a connection between the rise in A.D.D. diagnoses and the reduction in recreation time given to elementary school students. The study correlated the decrease in attention span time, with the increase in classroom time. In other words, a student can only sit in rows for a limited time before his or her attention, and passion, begins to drift. I fear the same thing is happening in our churches.

If church is nothing but sitting in rows while someone speaks, they will find something else to do. This generation is S.A.D.D. - they suffer from Spiritual Attention Deficit Disorder. They have nothing to do but sit and listen, so they throw their energy behind something that matters - something that's moving.

Recently, the world has seen a serious problem in Europe of young people flocking to the extremist Jihadist group known as ISIS. If interest in spiritual matters was on the global decline, then this movement of young people makes no sense.

Why the rush to recruitment?

Because young people are *not* disinterested in spiritual matters, only spiritual matters that don't move, that exist in theory, that are not incarnational. Globalism, which has brought all that the world has to offer to the fingertips and laptops of our children, has done the church a huge favor. It's convinced them that there has to be more, because what they're seeing isn't enough.

Spiritualism is "in." But only the brand that can touch and mark ourselves and others. This kind of movement - this generation would die to be a part of.

A Faith You Can Touch

"Faith without deeds is dead" – James 2:17

Young people are tired of a Faith you only "believe." They would rather have a Faith you can "touch," and that touches others. "Touching faith" is what convinces this generation that God is real and authentic, especially having grown up in a Hollywood-esque world where everything is Photoshopped and electronically enhanced. If Faith can touch and transform what it touches, they're in. So, let's give them something to touch.

The harvest is plentiful. There's more than enough work to go around. The world is in no shortage of pain and suffering. If, as parents, pastors, and leaders, we begin to present opportunities to our students, they will move, and own, their faith. No more "unemployed" students sitting in church with nothing to do. *Give faith a job, and it will work.*

I wonder: would the disciples have left their nets if Jesus' call to them had been: "Come, and be admirers of God"? He knew what He was doing when He said, "Come and be fishers of men." Jesus wasn't offering a religion or a philosophy - He was offering a job. Peter and John already had a *religion*, what they lacked was a *purpose*. I wonder how many "nets" our students would be willing to lay down if more leaders offered purpose? If you want to move a young person, *move* them.

VASQUEZ

PART 3

HAVE YOU MET HIM?

VASQUEZ

Chapter 11

I'M ALL OUT OF CHANGE

"You can do more than pray after you have prayed,

but you cannot do more than pray

until you have prayed."

– A. J. Gordon

"What if this doesn't work?"

Then, try something new.

"What if that doesn't work?"

Then, try something new.

"And if that doesn't work?"

Then, try something new.

I've always wanted to see young people meet Christ and be filled with His Spirit. I've always wanted to see our youth group grow. I want to see impact in my community. And I've spent thousands of dollars in conferences, books, and degrees trying to figure out how to do exactly that.

Every time I came back from a conference or class, or every time I've finished a book, I would try something new. *Change* is often a hallmark in youth ministry; we really don't give many things a chance before throwing them in the trash. If an idea doesn't work, no problem – we move on to the next great idea.

For a while, the changes work. But, eventually there comes a point where change ceases to be as effective as it once was. Then, the frustration sets in, because you feel like you don't have the resources necessary to achieve the results you know you're called to see. I think Peter can relate.

One day while on his way to the Temple, a crippled man stops him and asks for help, specifically for money. I love Peter's response: "Silver or gold I do not have, but what I have I give to you" (Acts 3:6). Peter is confronted with a situation, a dilemma, in which he does not have the physical or tangible capacity to meet the need. He has no money. So he says, "Sorry, I'm all out - of change."

I've been "out of change" before. Have you? It's a dark place. There's a sense of hopelessness - because you've come to what feels like "the end." You know it's just not going to work. You've tried everything. What do you do then? When you've become exhausted from moving from strategy to strategy? From fad to fad? When you're out of change?

"But What I HAVE I Give to You..."

What did Peter have? At first glance, not much. We know that aside from Jesus, he had no formal ministry training. We also know his ministerial track record was not the sharpest. He never displayed the intellect of Paul or the intimacy of John the Beloved. Peter couldn't lead like James, and - not to mention - he's broke. He had no resources. But, what he did have, he received in an upper room a few weeks earlier: the power and presence of the Holy Spirit coursing through his veins. And it was enough, even more than enough.

If you're at the end of your rope, you're right where God wants you — all out of change. Once you're there, you're forced to look on high for your next step. Because when all else fails, God doesn't.

Maybe everything else failed, because God was trying to tell you something: You can't do it without Him. So go get Him. Because, like Peter said, you can only give what you have.

I was tempted to put this chapter at the beginning of this book.

Because it's the first thing you need to do. Have you ever been in a conversation with someone who has been battling an illness? I've often heard this person say, once the medicine doesn't work, and the doctor is out of options, "Well, I guess all that's left to do is pray." As if prayer were some sort of last resort. As if it were a thing to do when nothing else works. If that's true, it's only because we turn to prayer when nothing else works, but not because it doesn't work. Prayer works! Fasting works! Pursuing God's presence works. Not just as a last resort - but as a first priority.

I weep internally at the response I get from youth pastors when they ask me why God has been blessing our youth ministry. "So what are you guys doing in Orlando that's creating such success?"

"Prayer," I say.

"But what else are you doing?" they ask.

"What else? Working, of course. Working hard. Are you?"

"Yes, but it's not working."

"Then pray! Pray hard!"

What strategies did the disciples employ? Or Abraham? Or Elijah? Yes, there are approaches, theories, styles, methods, and marketing tactics to be researched; if you're not doing and studying all that, then start studying and doing. Learn how to be a better parent, how to be a better pastor, how to be a better person. But, if you've tried it all, and you're still not seeing the results you want, then pray. Or better yet: pray before you try *any* of it, *while* you execute it, and *after* you've evaluated it.

"Prayer is the first thing, the second thing, the third thing necessary to a minister. Pray, then, my dear brother; pray, pray, pray". - Edward Payson

I finally settled on placing this chapter here, at the end, because prayer isn't just the first thing you do; more importantly, it's the next thing you do. It's what you do right after you've failed. It's what you do right after you've won. It's what you do when your kids graduate high school. It's what you do when they drop out. It's what you do when your youth group is growing. It's what you do when no one's coming. And most immediately, *it's what you do the moment you put this book down.*

When Peter had nothing else - when he was all out of change - it was the one thing he knew he had. How about you? Are you confident in your "spiritual bank account?" Have you made any deposits lately? Don't get me wrong. I believe in grace - as some put it, "Jesus is the one who does it." (Amen). He's the one who makes me righteous. But, James doesn't tell us that the prayers of a righteous man are effective. He tells us that the *fervent* prayers of a righteous man are effective (James 5:16). Jesus makes me righteous, but I must be fervent. That word translated is *"Energeo"* - which means to put forth effort and work.

Peter put the effort and work into prayer. He made the necessary investments in his alone time. He wasn't confident in his resources; he had none. He was "God-fident" in his relationship with the Maker. You have to put the time, effort, and work into prayer - or this generation will be left to find God on their own, and encounter many false gods along the way.

Have You Met Him?

Social laws dictate that you cannot introduce someone to a person you've never met. I can introduce you to my wife, my pastor, and my friends, but I can't introduce you to someone I don't have a relationship with. If you want to introduce this generation to the God of the universe, you must have met Him first for yourself. So, have you met Him?

If not, then every chapter before this was for you. But if you've met Him, and somewhere along the line your relationship faded - as things that are not tended to often do - then reawaken the love. Don't simply "remember" the day you met Him. We can rarely draw the necessary motivation we need for the present out of the past. Nostalgia only leads to frustrating comparisons. In your mind, the "best" days will always be "yesterdays." Instead, pursue a new encounter today.

Only two chapters pass between Acts 2 and Acts 4; only two chapters before the disciples are in need of a spiritual renewal and refreshment. In Acts 2, they were all filled with the Spirit and began ministering in the power of God. But by Acts 4, the hardships of life have them in need again of a new encounter. God is like that, I fear. He's a fountain of living water - He never runs out. But, we must make the journey to the fountain, and drink. So, make your way to the fountain. Make your way to Bethel. You know where it is.

It's the distance from your knees to the floor.

Go there, please. A generation is counting on it.

He's lived in stories long enough.

It's time they *met* Him.

It's time to say *Hello.*

VASQUEZ

ABOUT THE AUTHOR

JJ Vasquez is a New York City native\Florida transplant who has been travelling and preaching the gospel since he was 12 years old. His desire to bring others into a real relationship with Christ led him to co-found a discipleship school, *Ignite*, at the age of 19. At 22 he was elected the District Youth Director of the Florida Multicultural District of the Assemblies of God, charged with the responsibility of training over 240 different churches and their respective leaders in reaching the next generation, also organizing statewide camps and conventions that drew thousands of people each year. Two years later he was hired as the Youth Pastor of *IEC Church* in Orlando FL, one of the largest multicultural churches in the nation, reaching over 4,000 people on a weekly basis. There he started a weekly podcast of his sermons that today have reached over 10,000 listeners in 15 different countries. With a heart for raising up leaders, he currently serves as the Assistant Professor of Youth and Family Ministry at *Southeastern University* in Lakeland, FL. JJ holds degrees in Religion, Political Science, Ministerial Leadership, and Divinity from the University of Florida, SEU, and Southwestern University. When he's not teaching, preaching, writing, or travelling, he's watching football with his two sons, Justice James, Zane Micah, and his wife Liz (the only one not watching football).

CPSIA information can be obtained
at www.ICGtesting.com
Printed in the USA
LVHW081819140120
643594LV00018B/1792